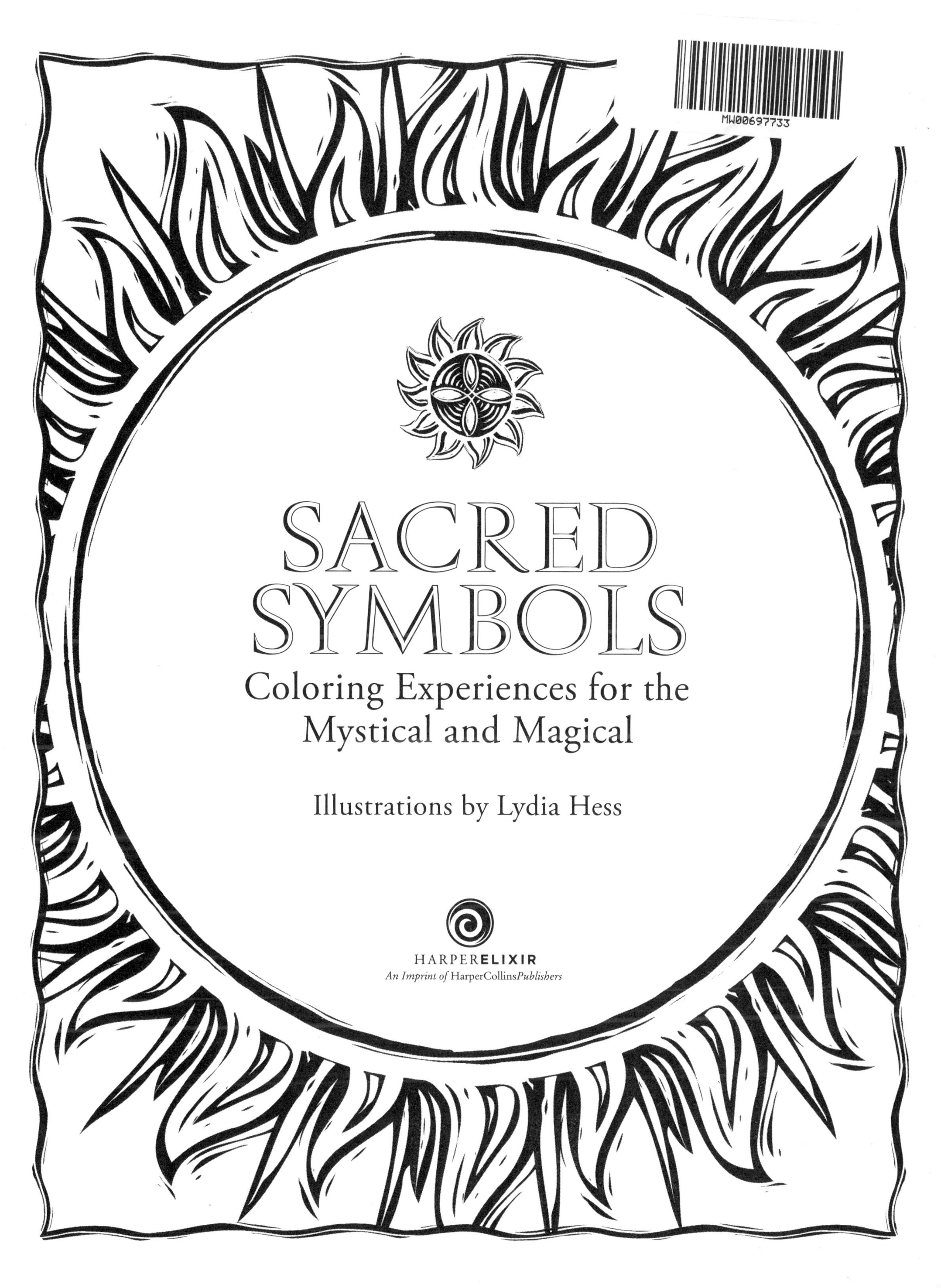

SACRED SYMBOLS

Coloring Experiences for the Mystical and Magical

Illustrations by Lydia Hess

HARPERELIXIR
An Imprint of HarperCollins*Publishers*

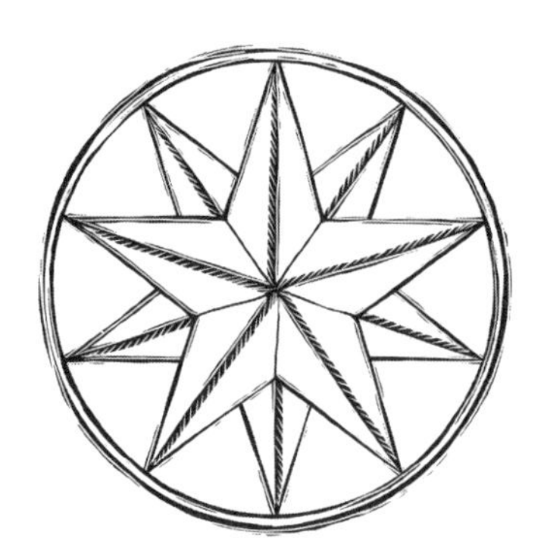

HarperCollins books may be purchased for educational, business, or sales promotional use.
For information please e-mail the Special Markets Department at SPsales@harpercollins.com.

HarperCollins website: http://www.harpercollins.com

FIRST EDITION

Designed by Lydia Hess

Library of Congress Cataloging-in-Publication Data is available upon request.
ISBN 978–0–06–243425–8

15 16 17 18 19 RRD(H) 10 9 8 7 6 5 4

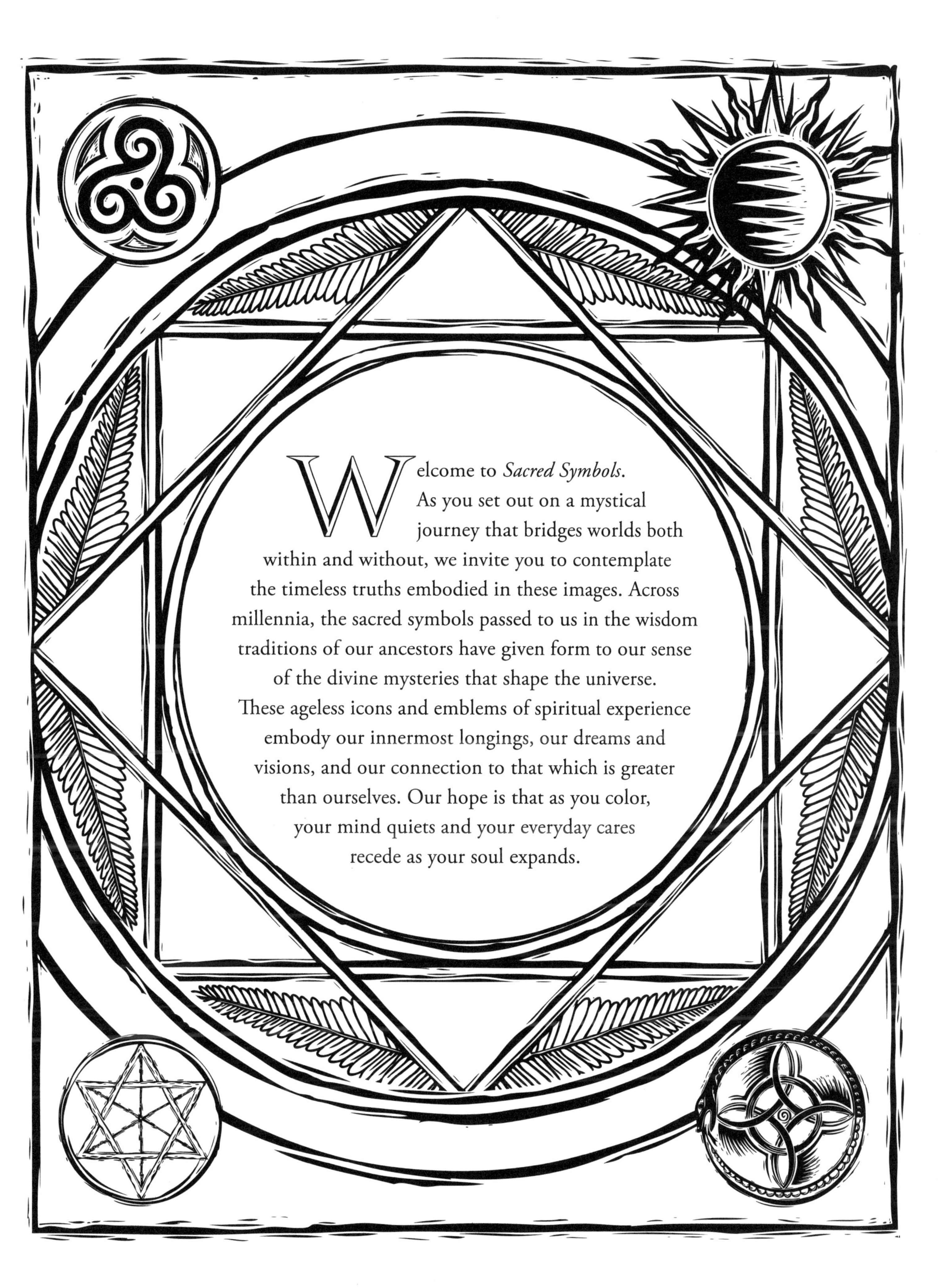

Welcome to *Sacred Symbols*. As you set out on a mystical journey that bridges worlds both within and without, we invite you to contemplate the timeless truths embodied in these images. Across millennia, the sacred symbols passed to us in the wisdom traditions of our ancestors have given form to our sense of the divine mysteries that shape the universe. These ageless icons and emblems of spiritual experience embody our innermost longings, our dreams and visions, and our connection to that which is greater than ourselves. Our hope is that as you color, your mind quiets and your everyday cares recede as your soul expands.

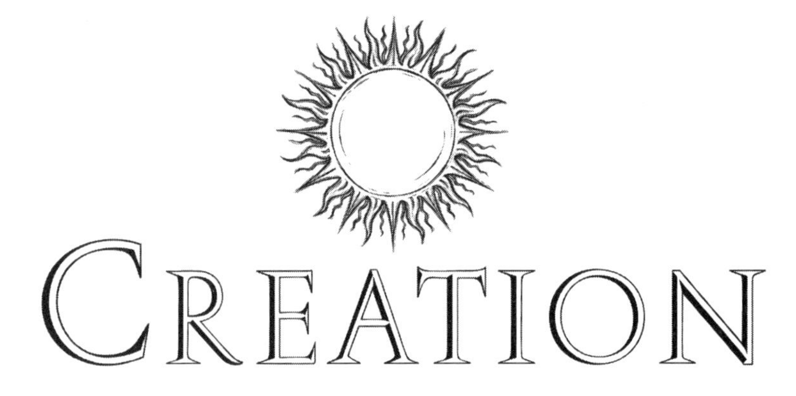
CREATION

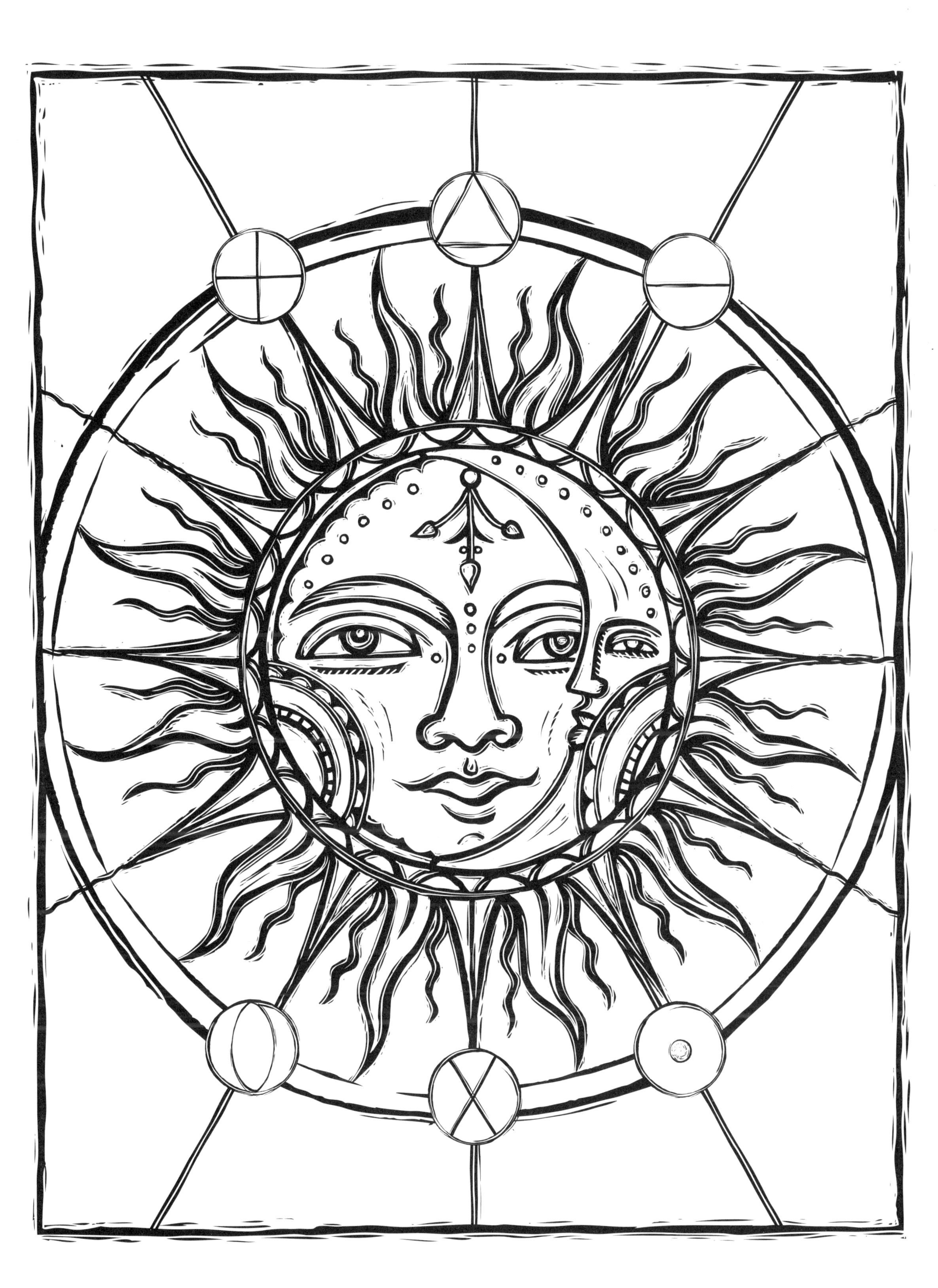

CYCLES

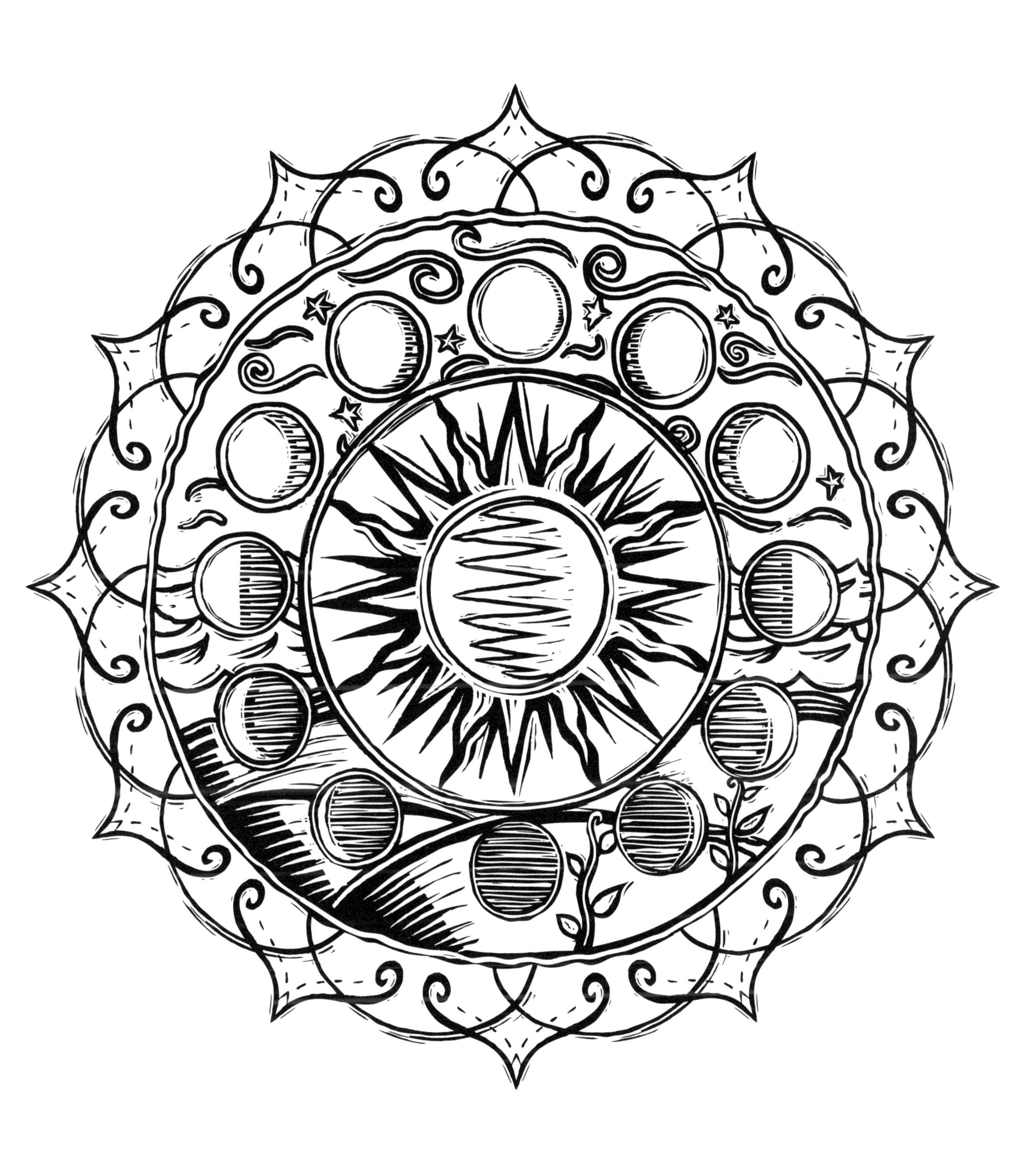

HARMONY

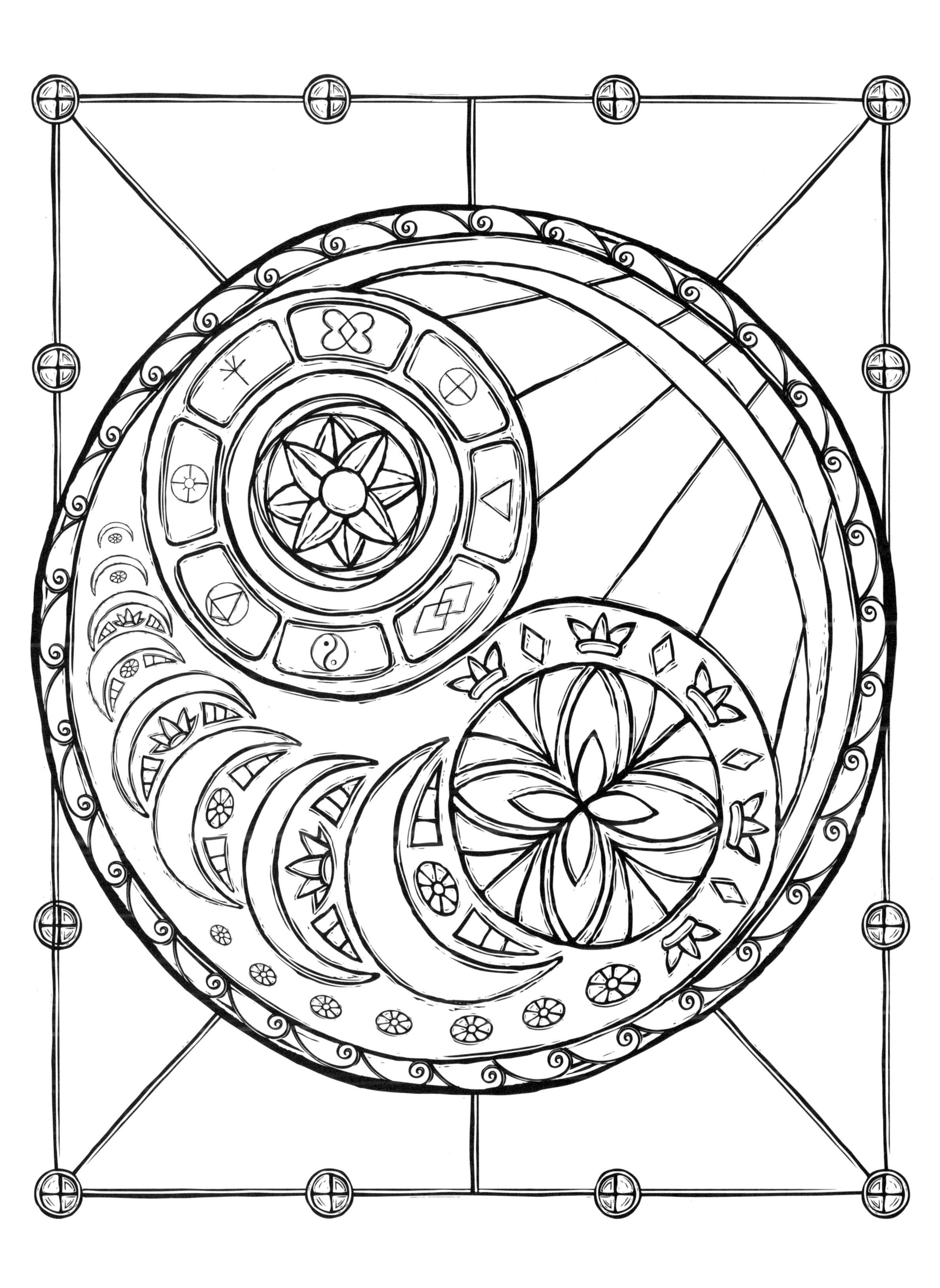

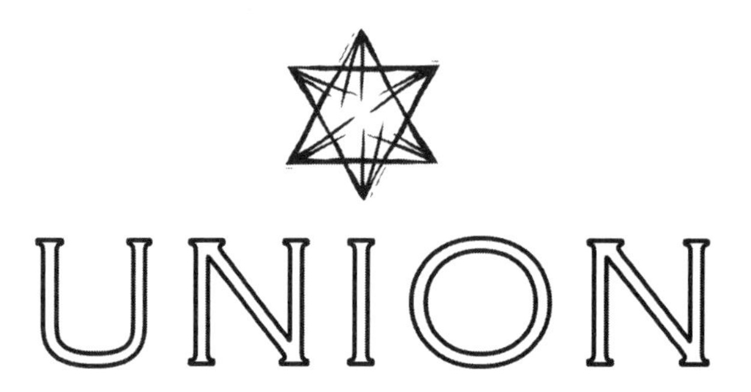
UNION

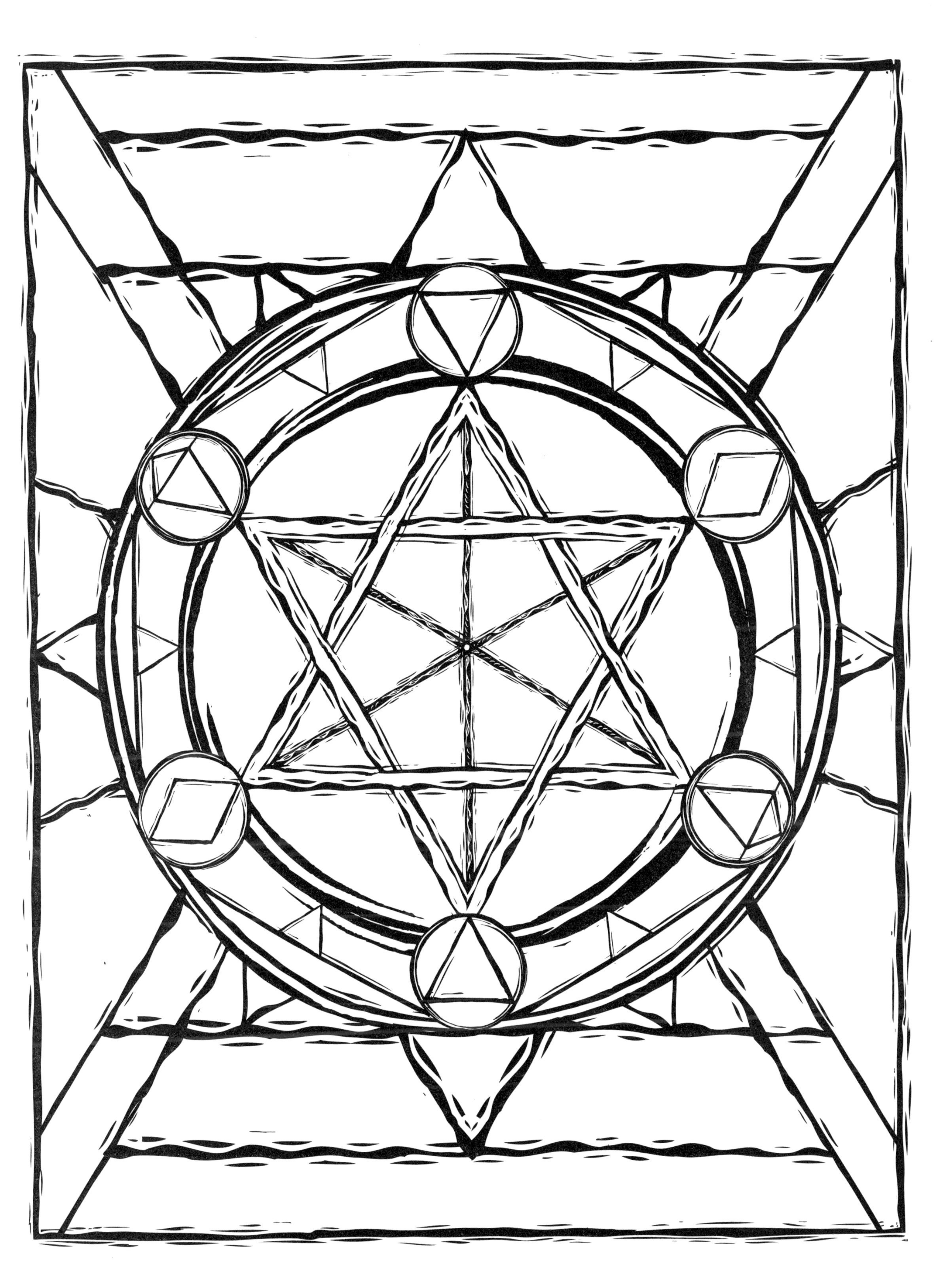

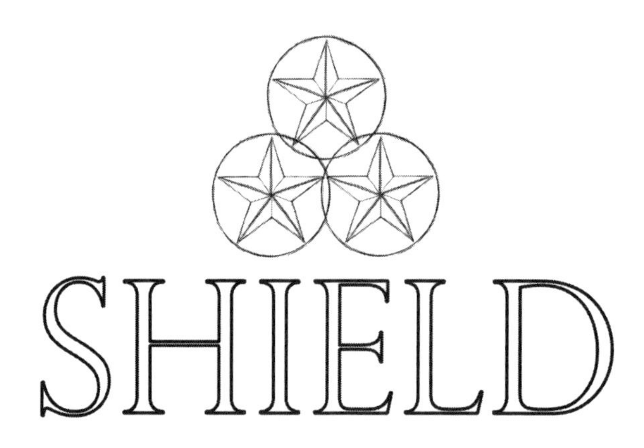
SHIELD

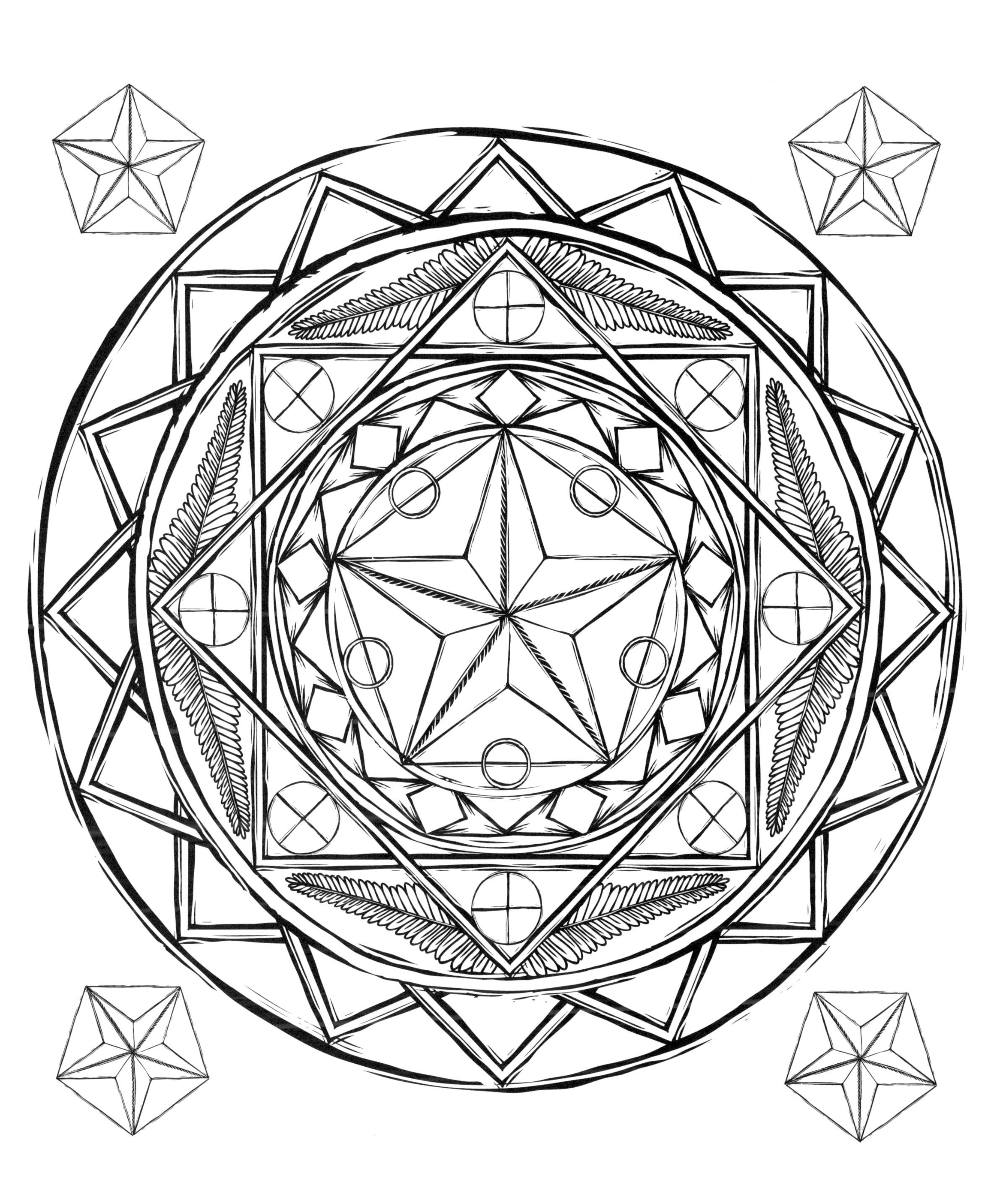

ascend

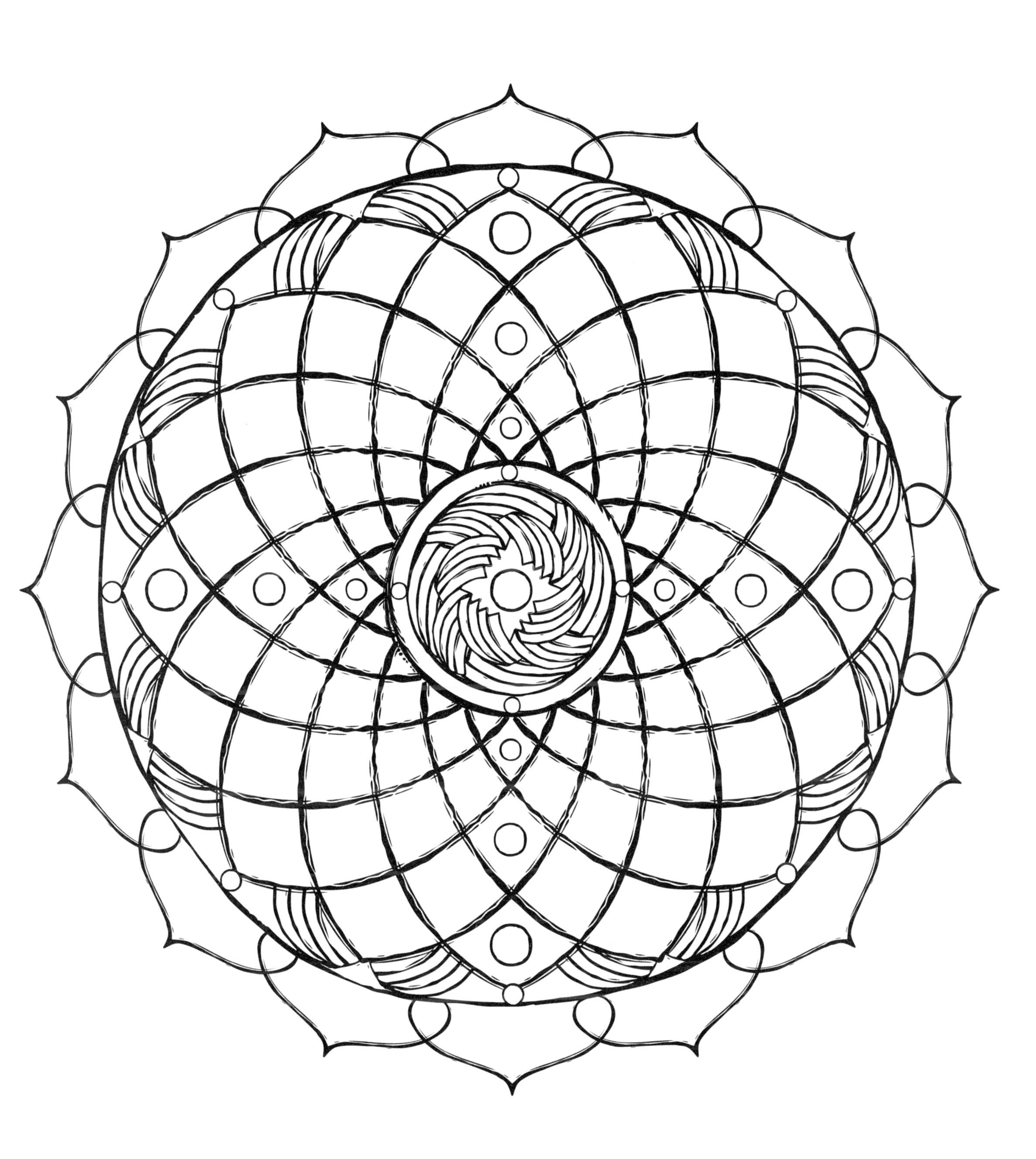

Spheres

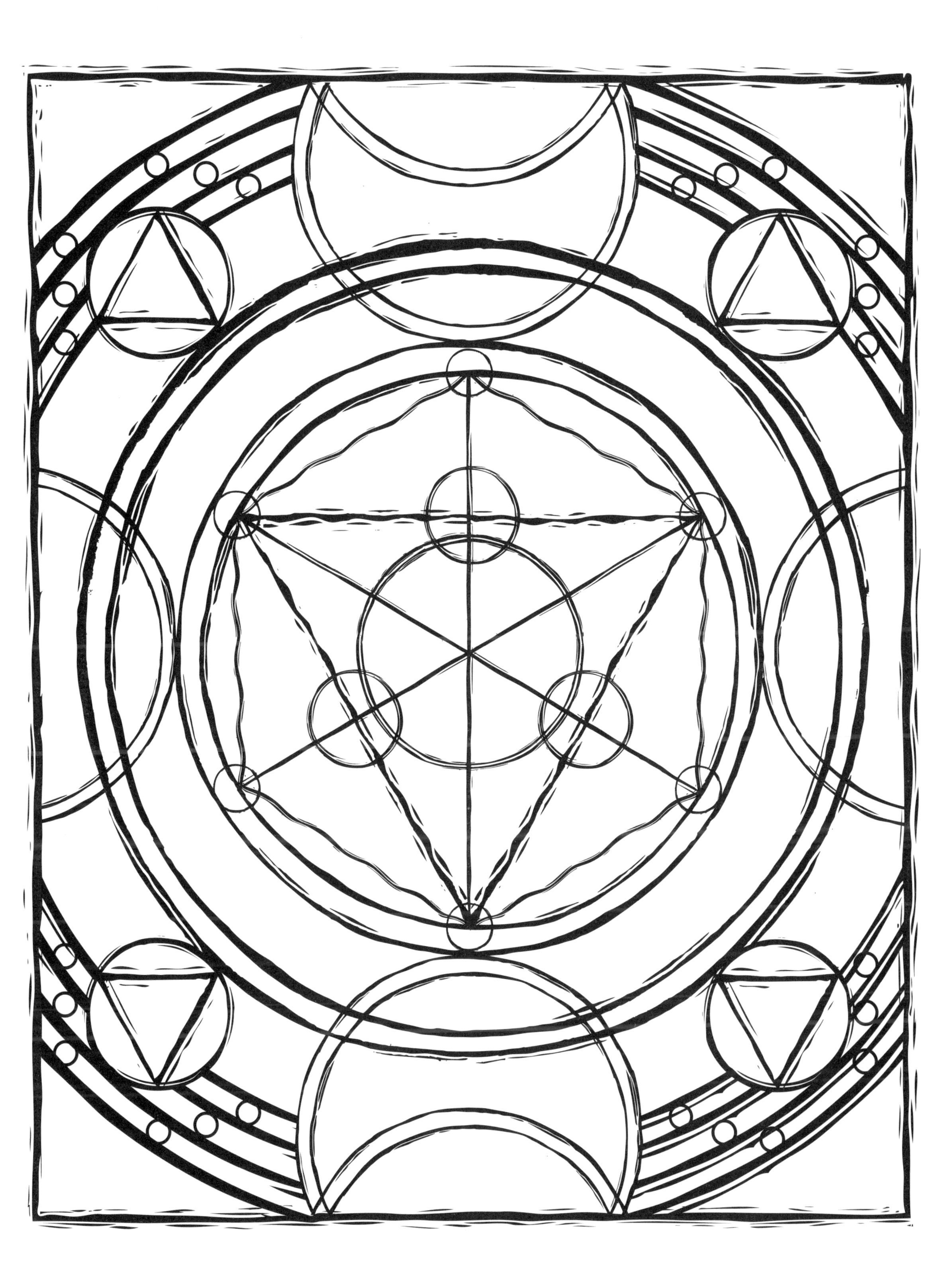

Dimensions

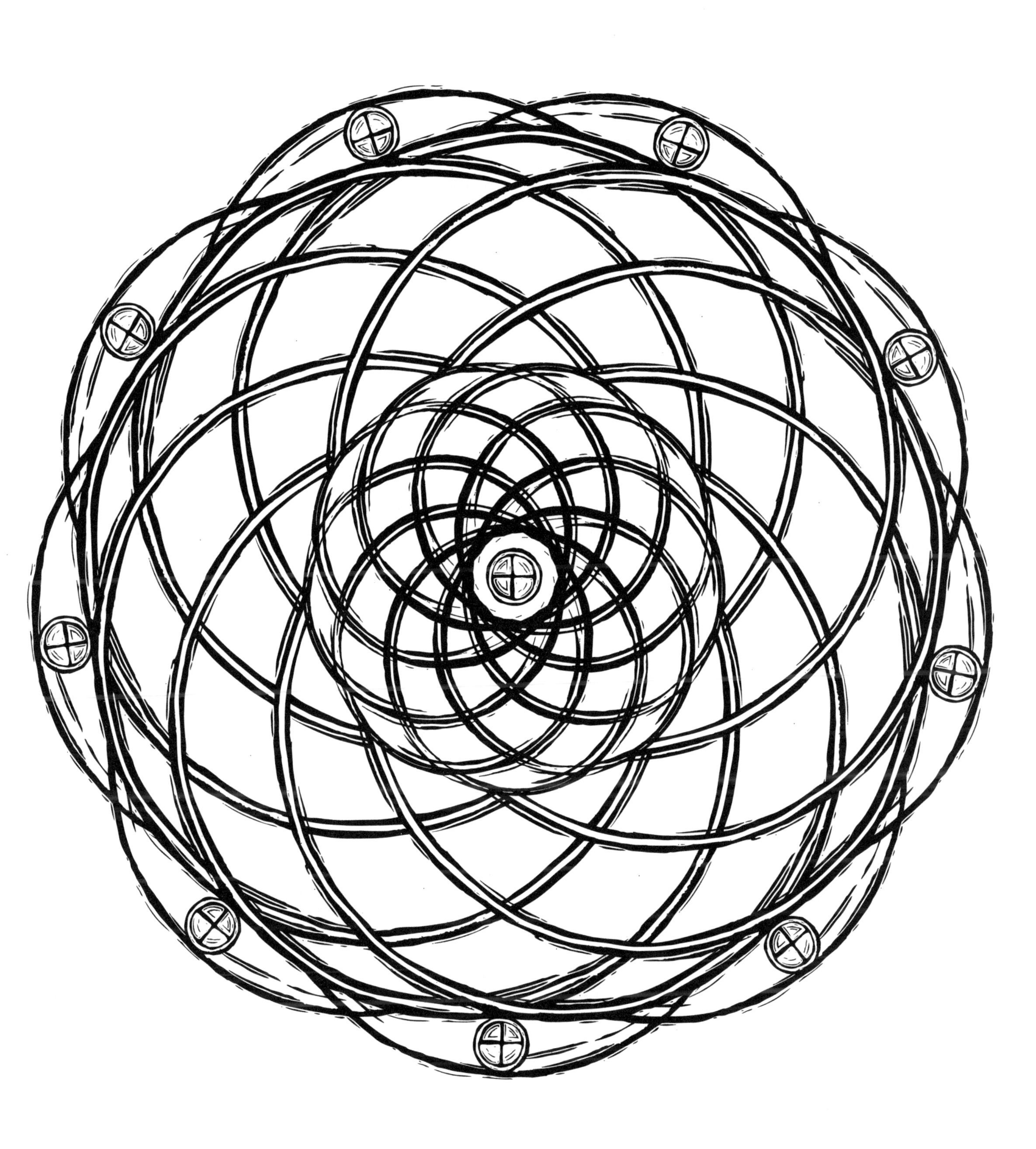

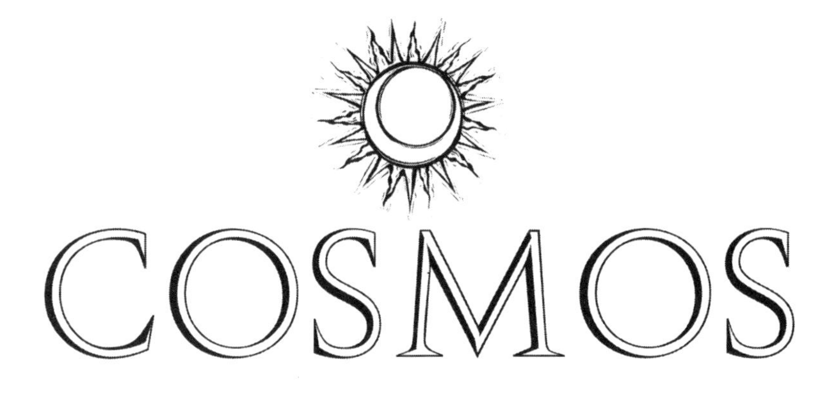
COSMOS

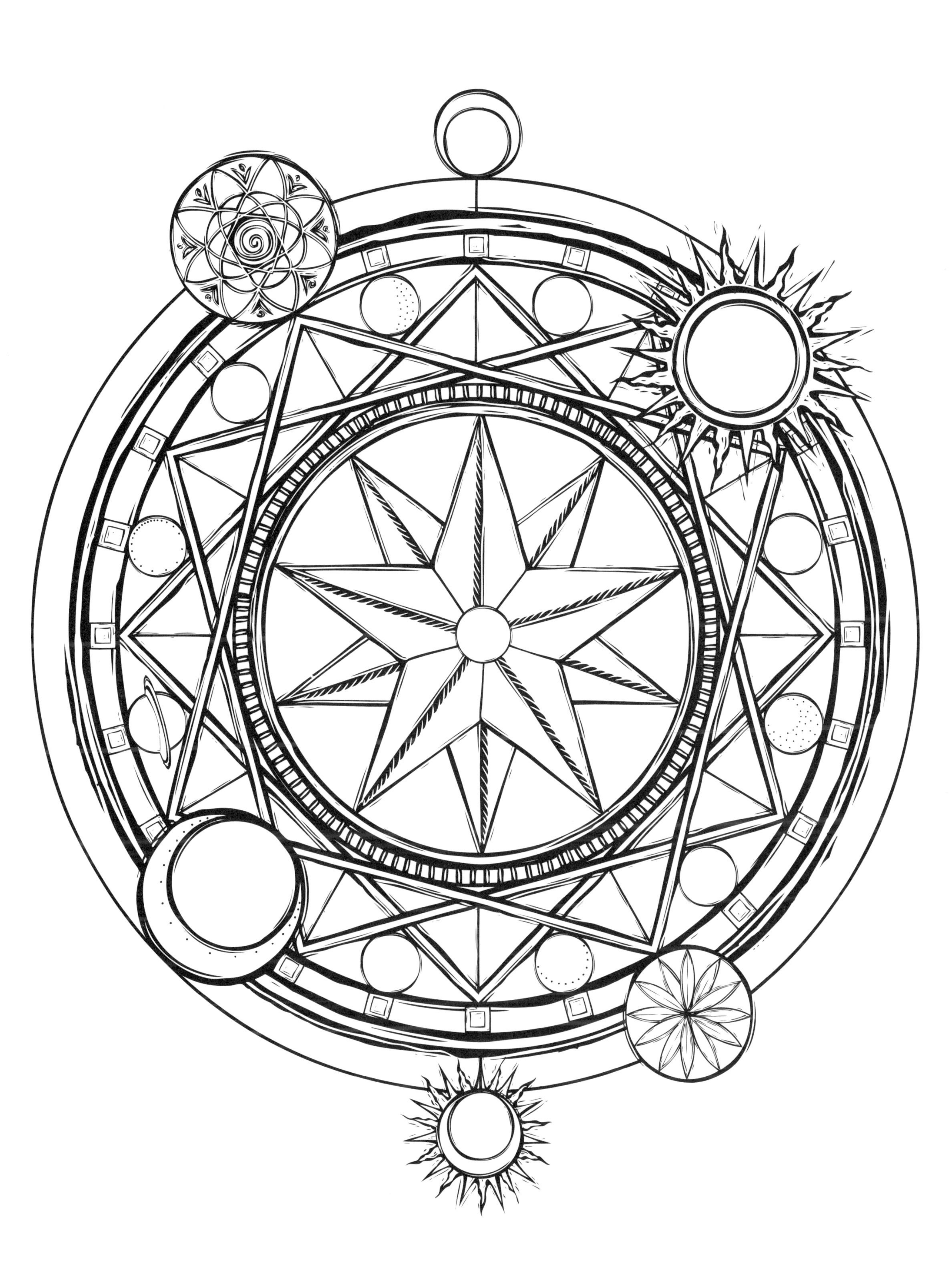

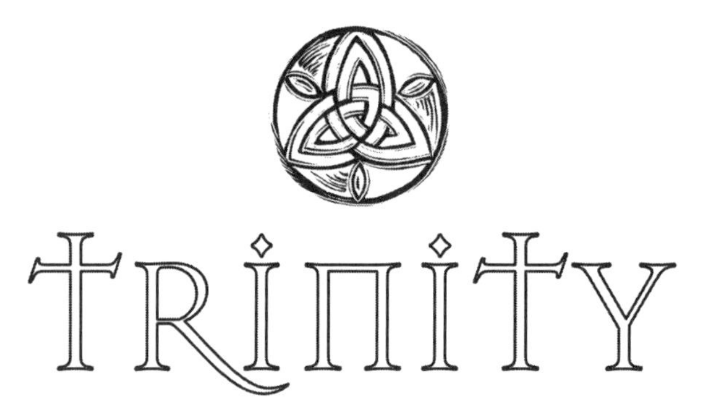
TRINITY

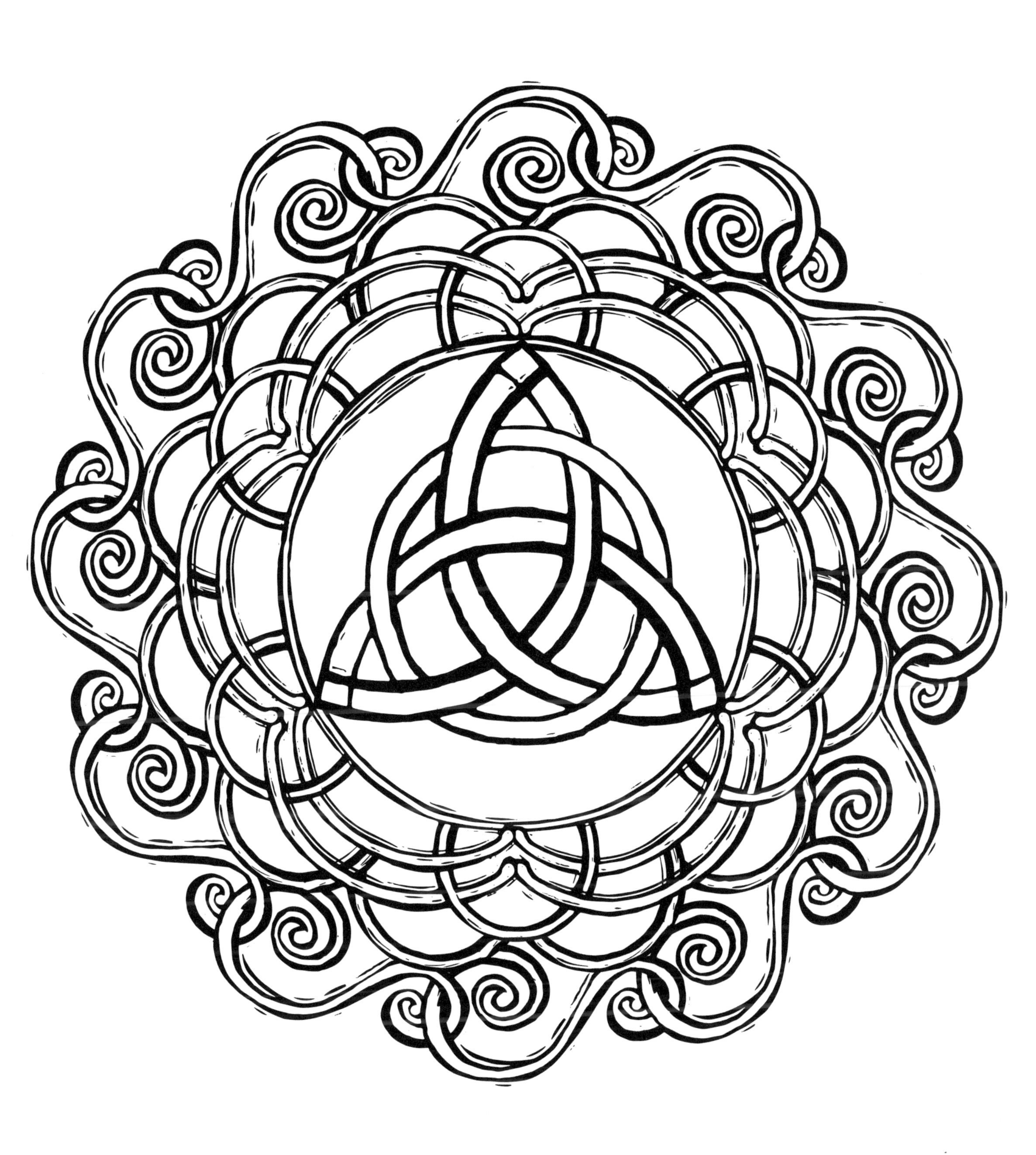

Continual

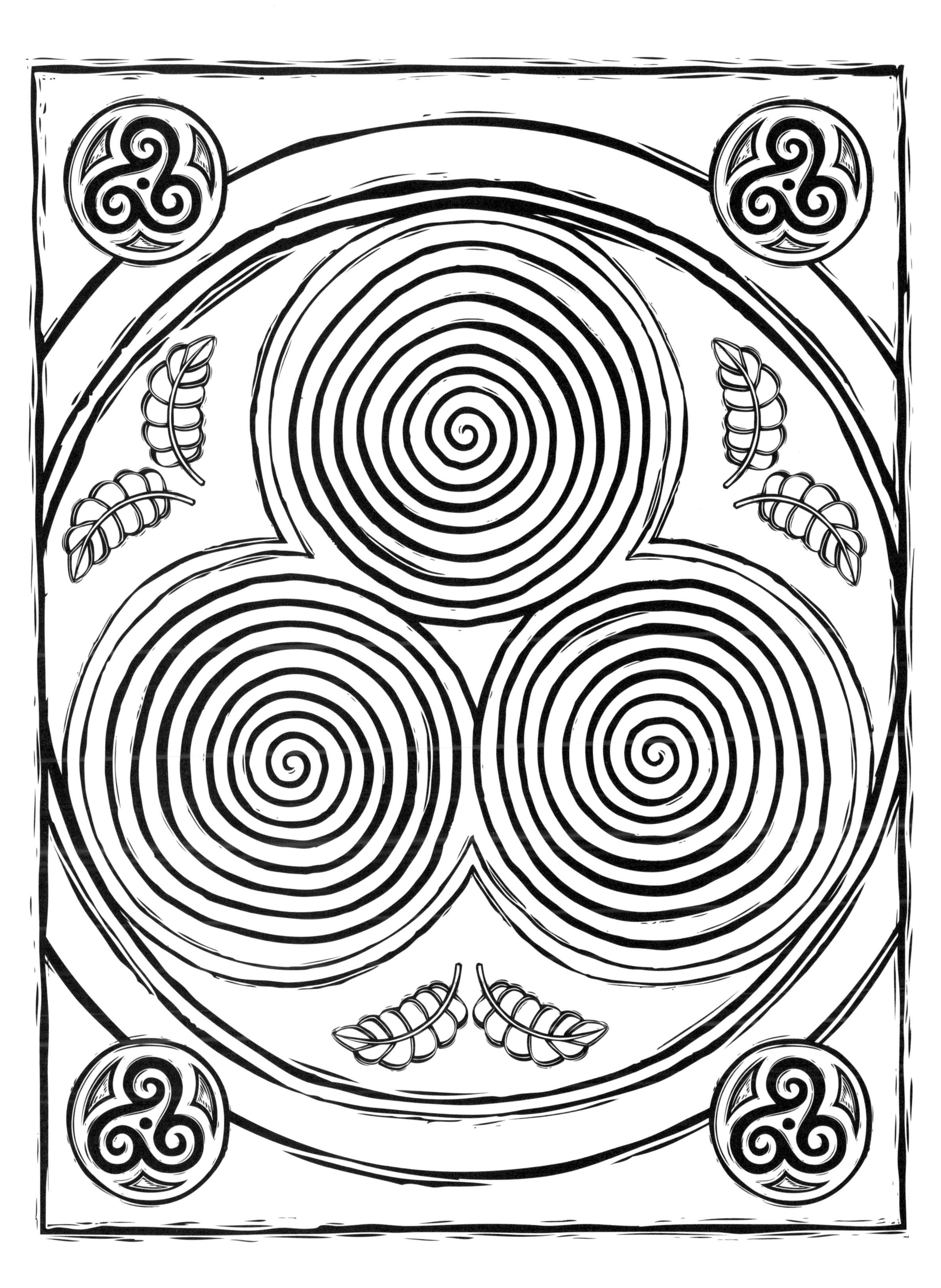

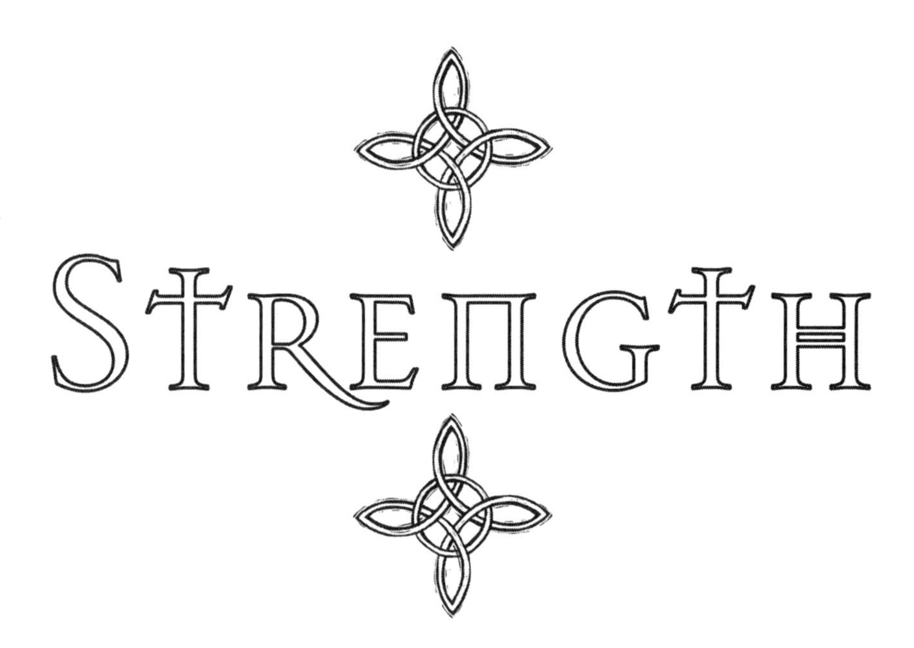
STRENGTH

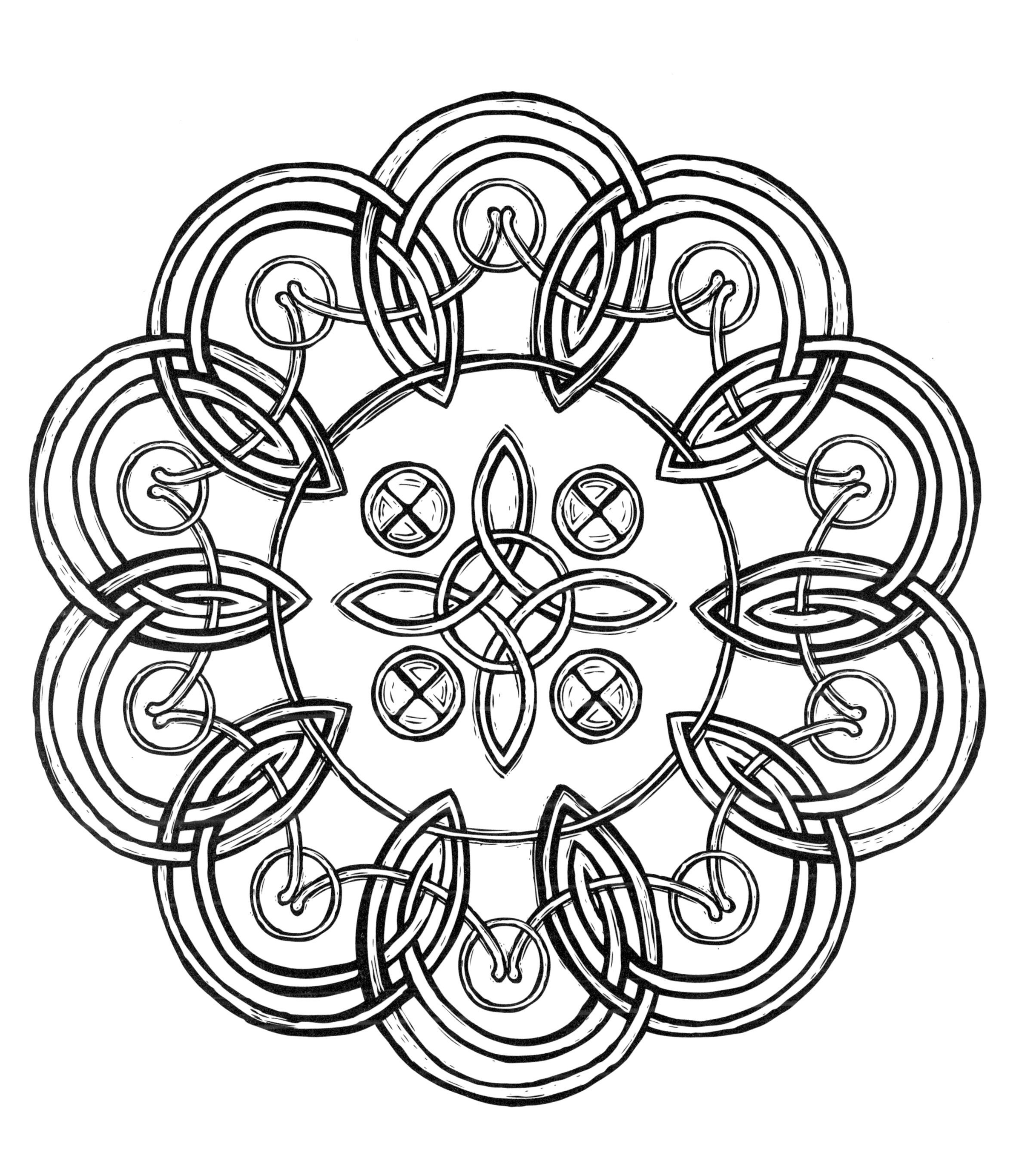

Foundation

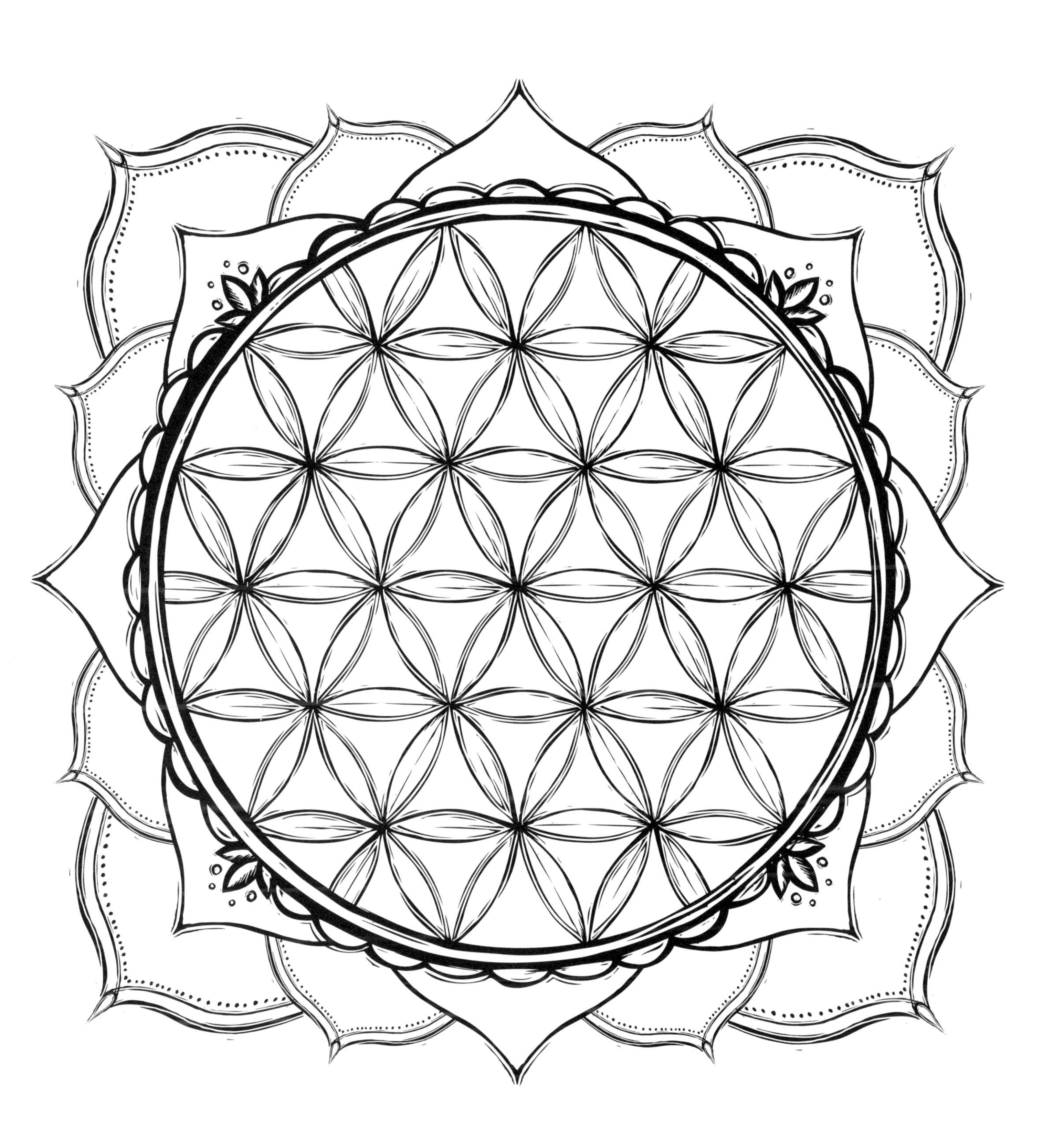

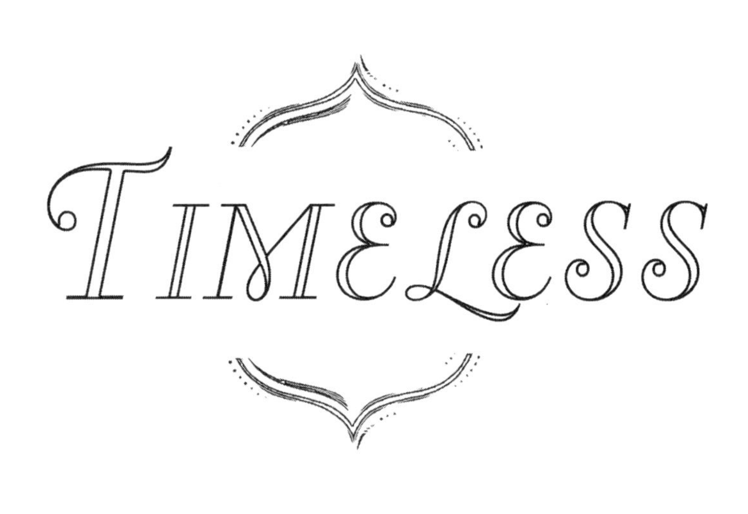
TIMELESS

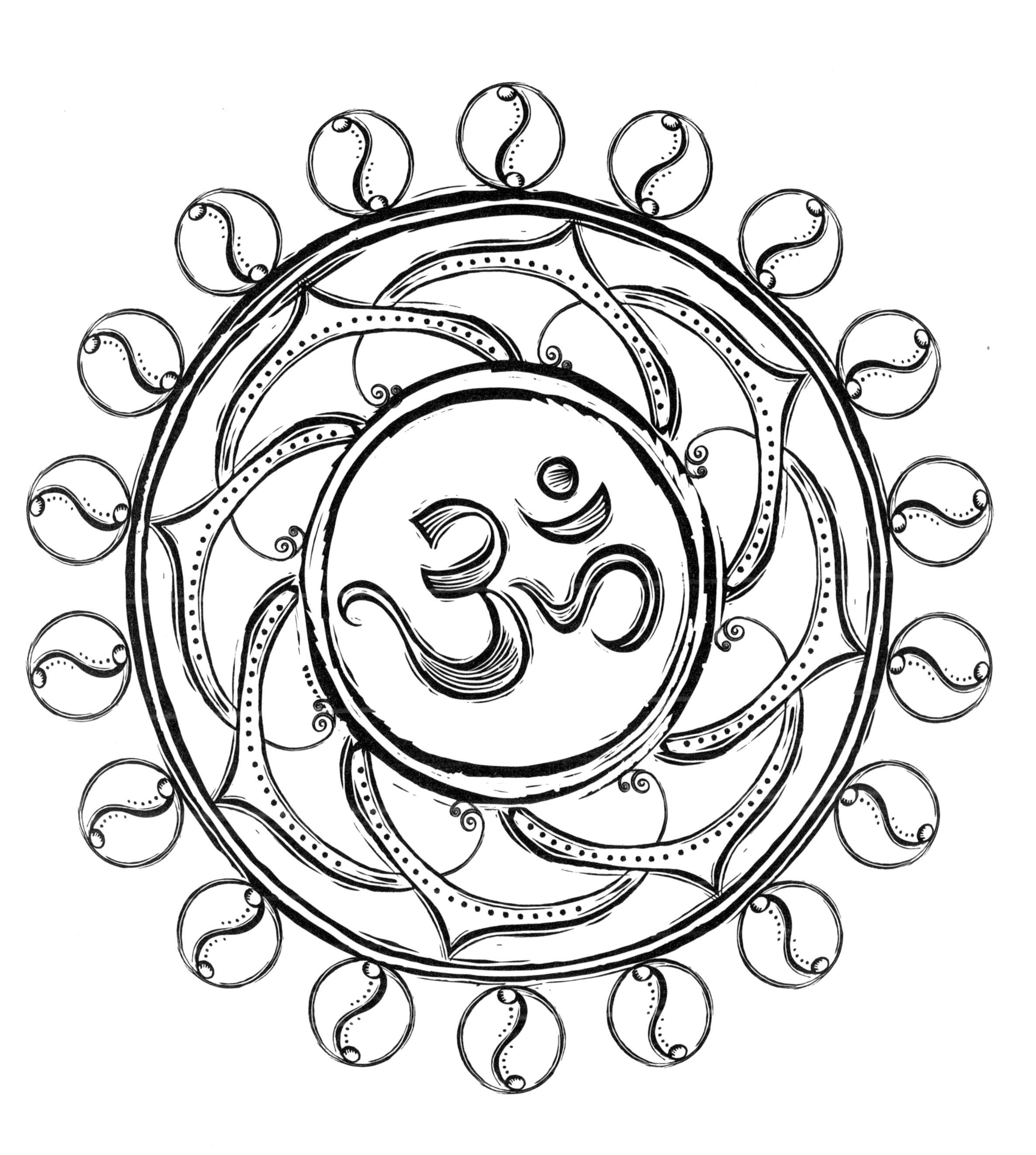

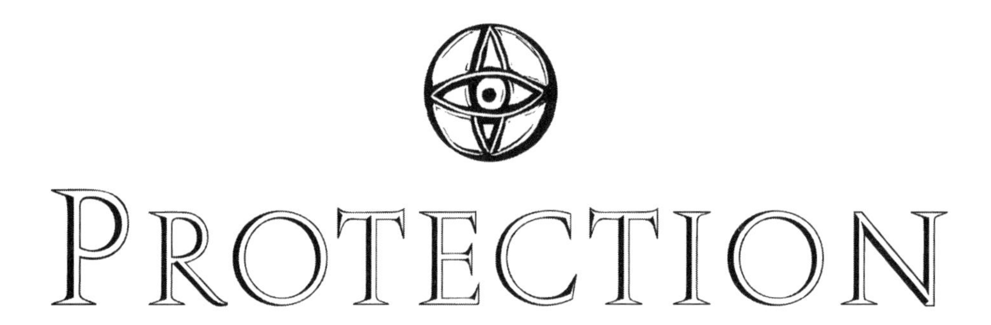

PROTECTION

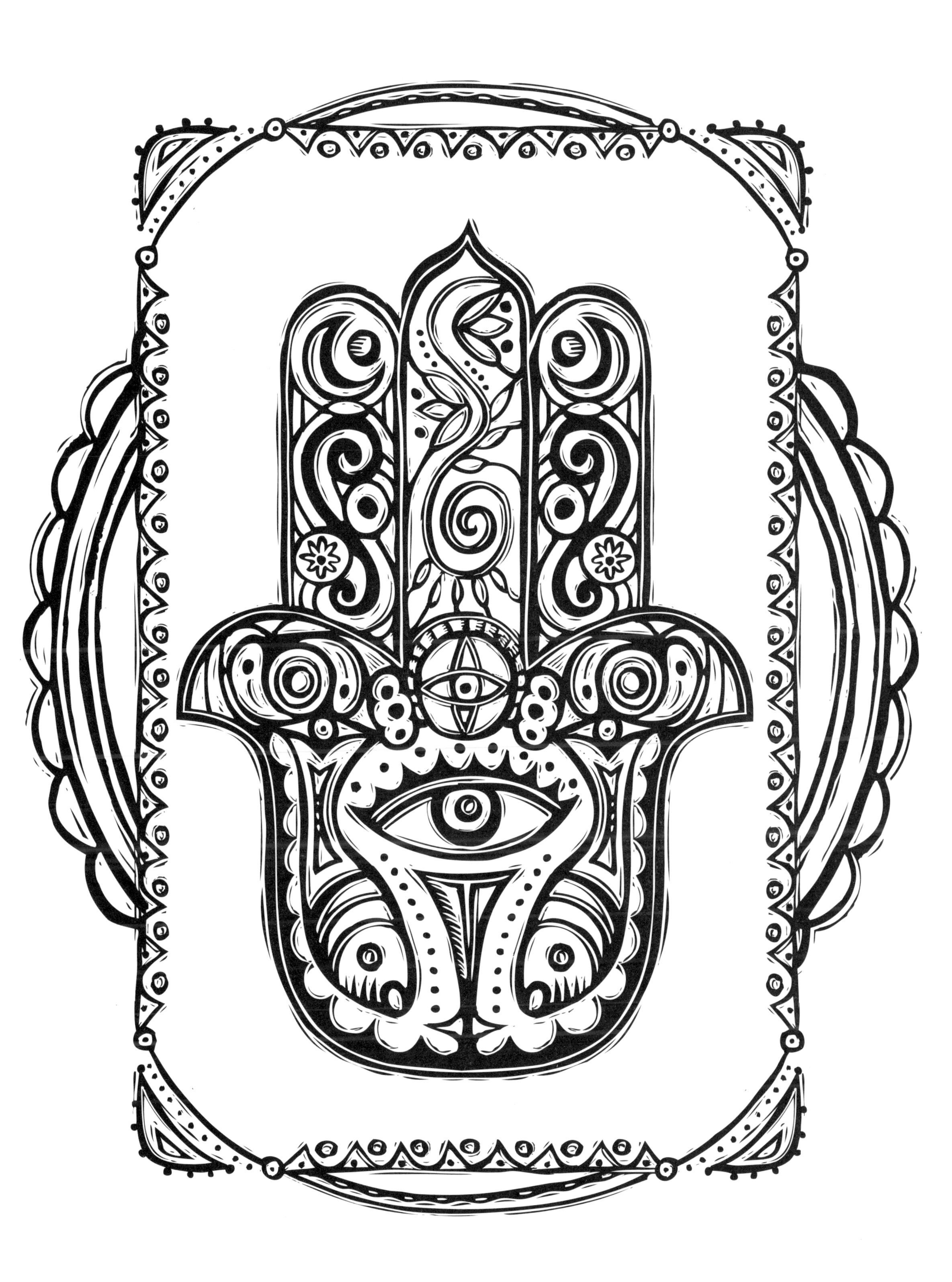

Prosperity

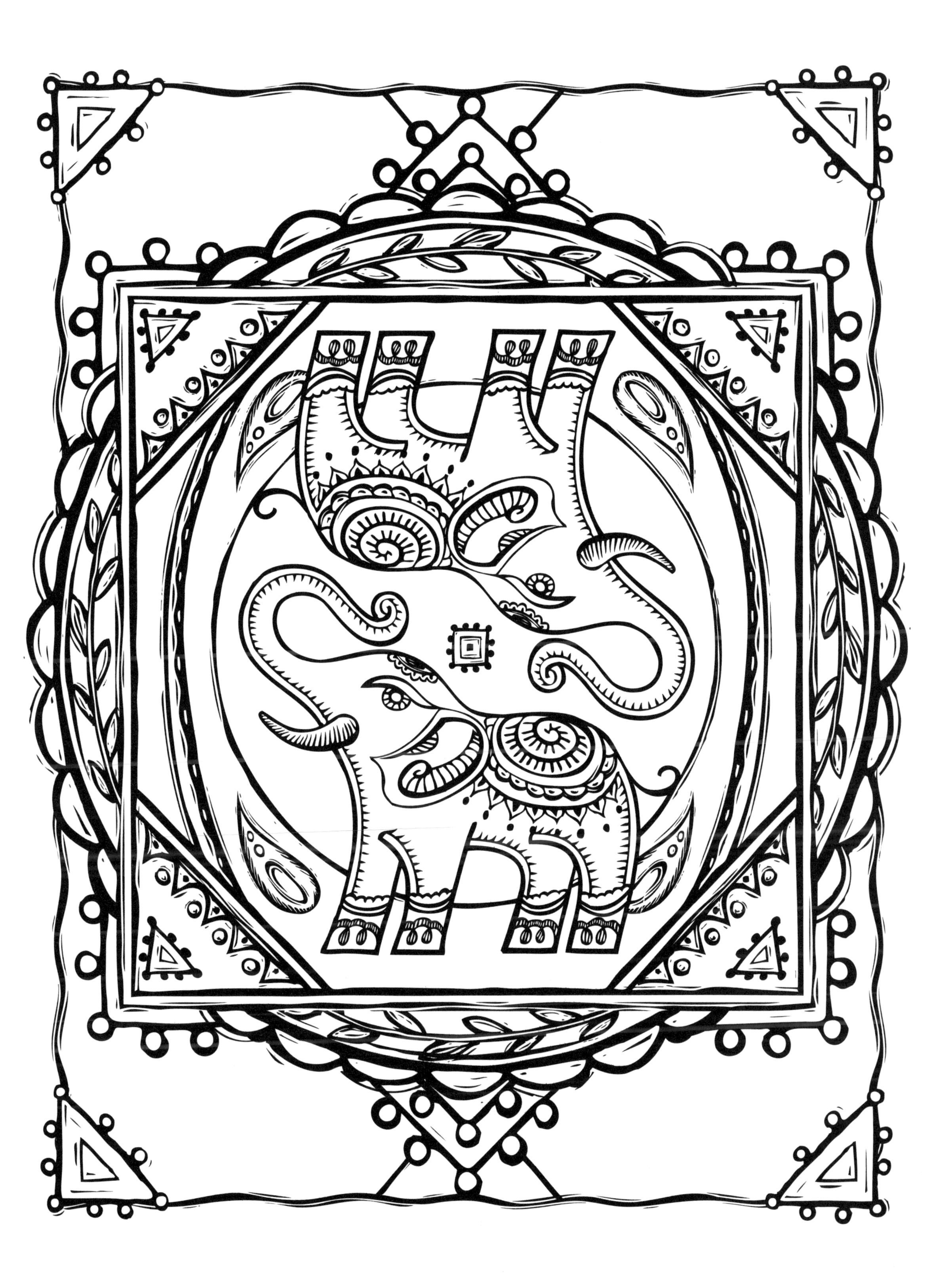

Symmetry

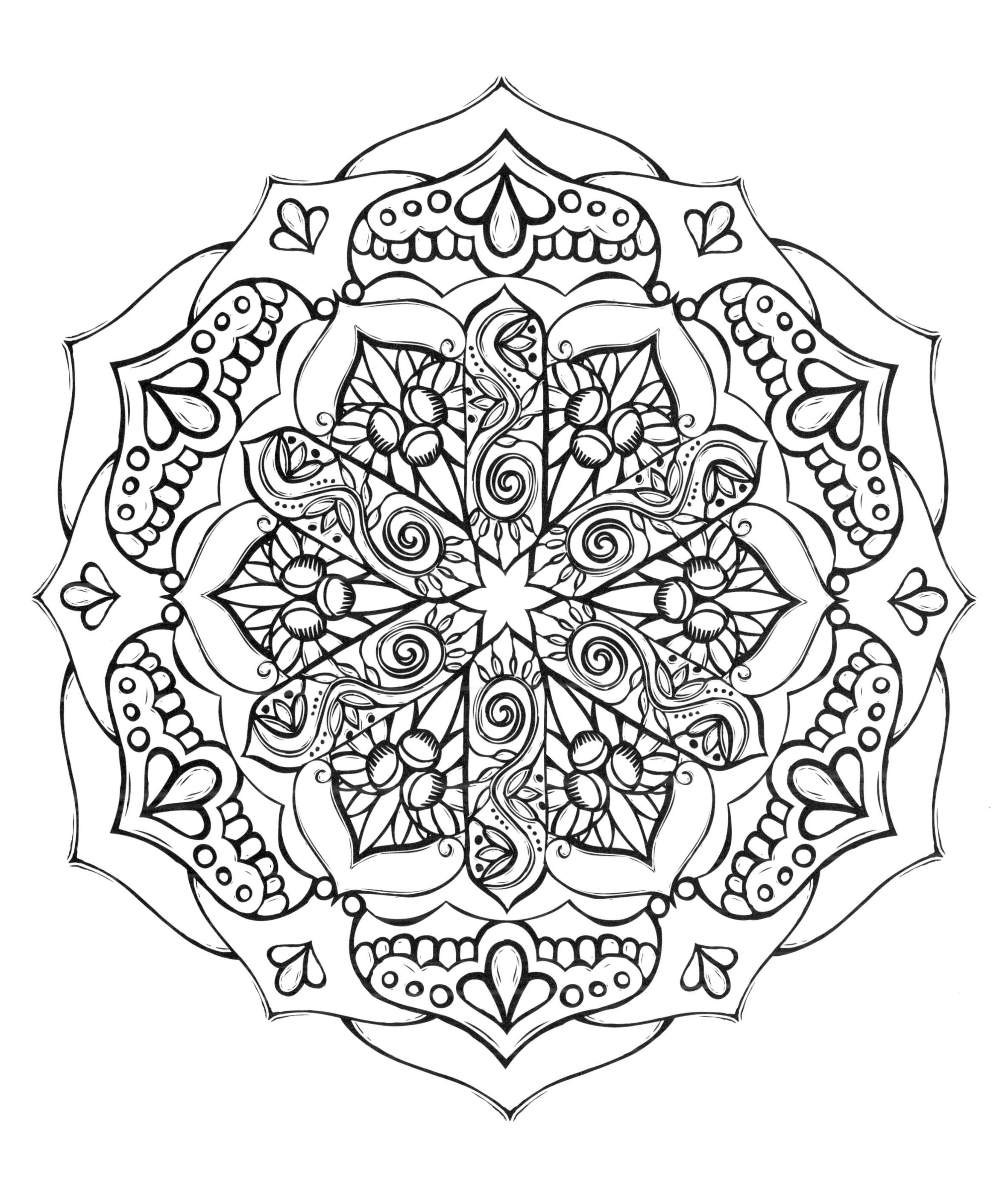

Awakening

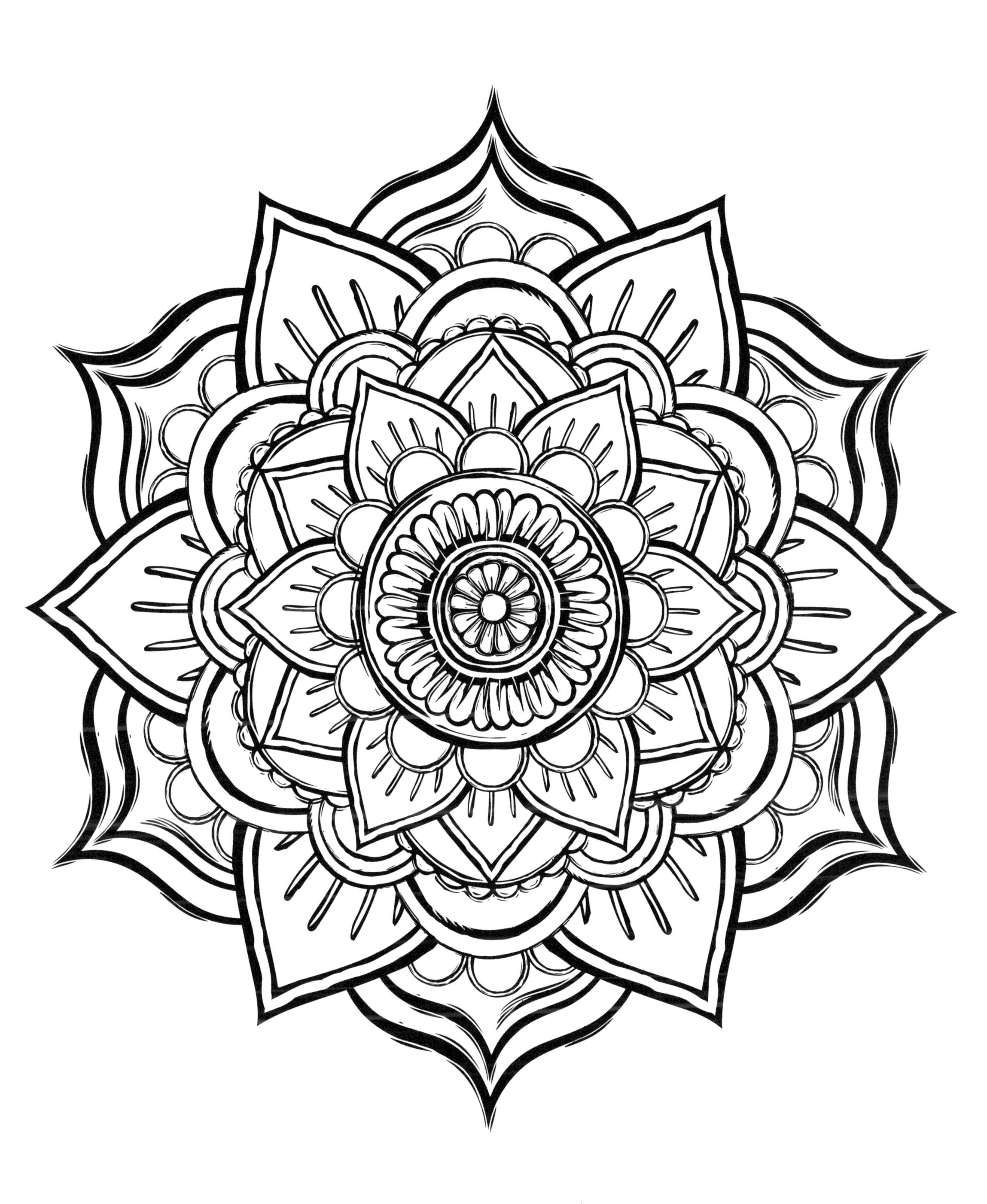

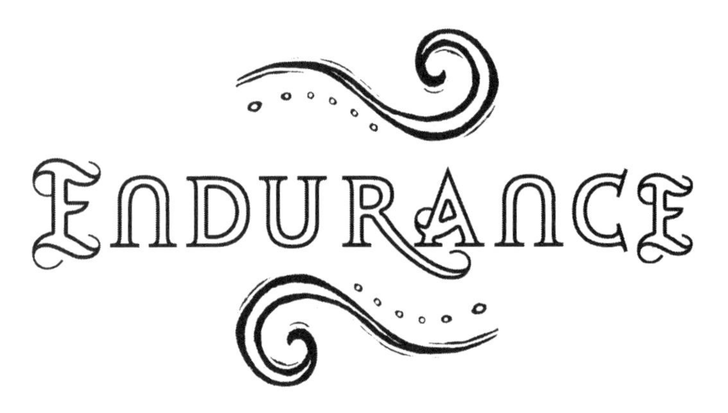
ENDURANCE

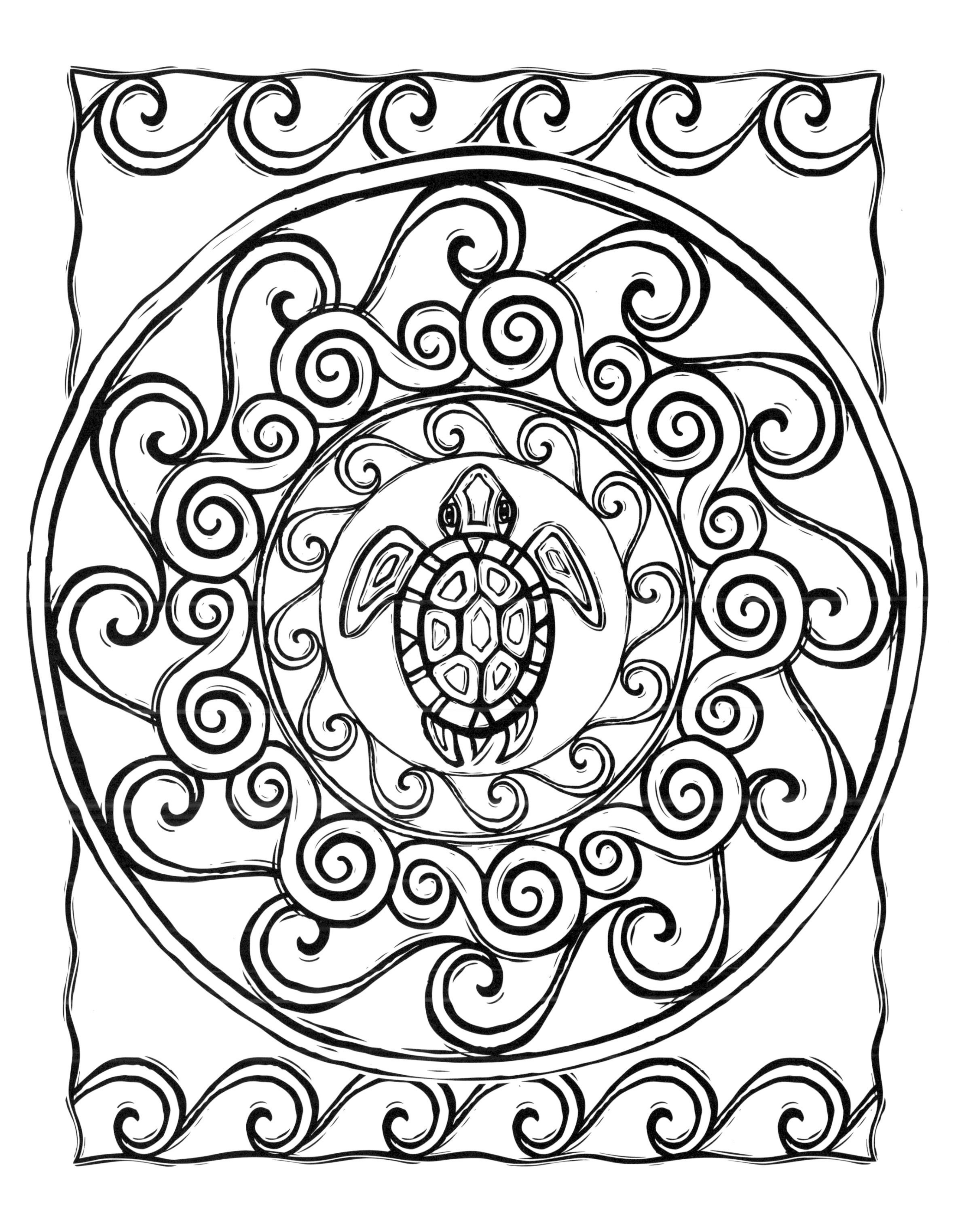

Interconnection

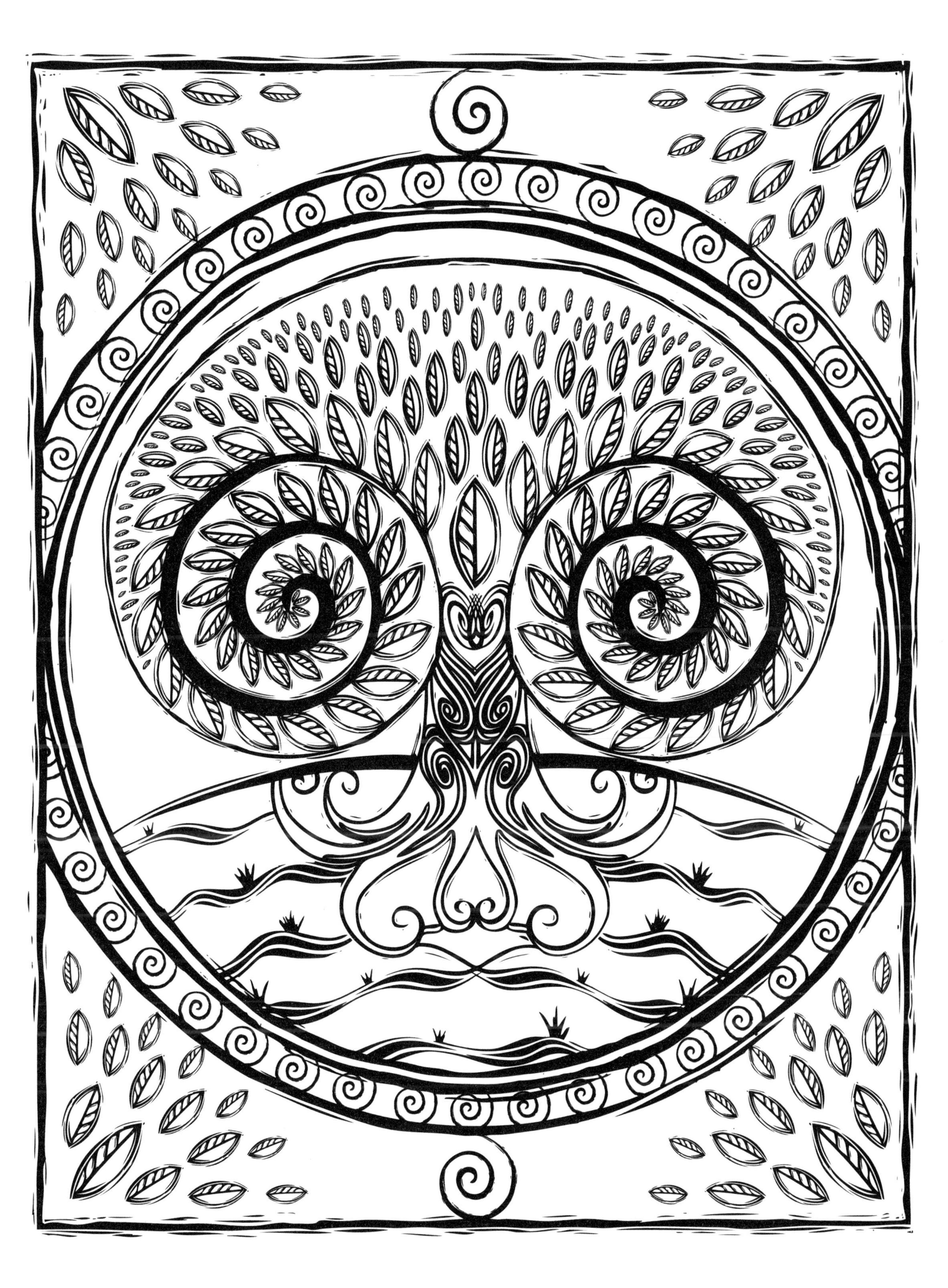

Fidelity

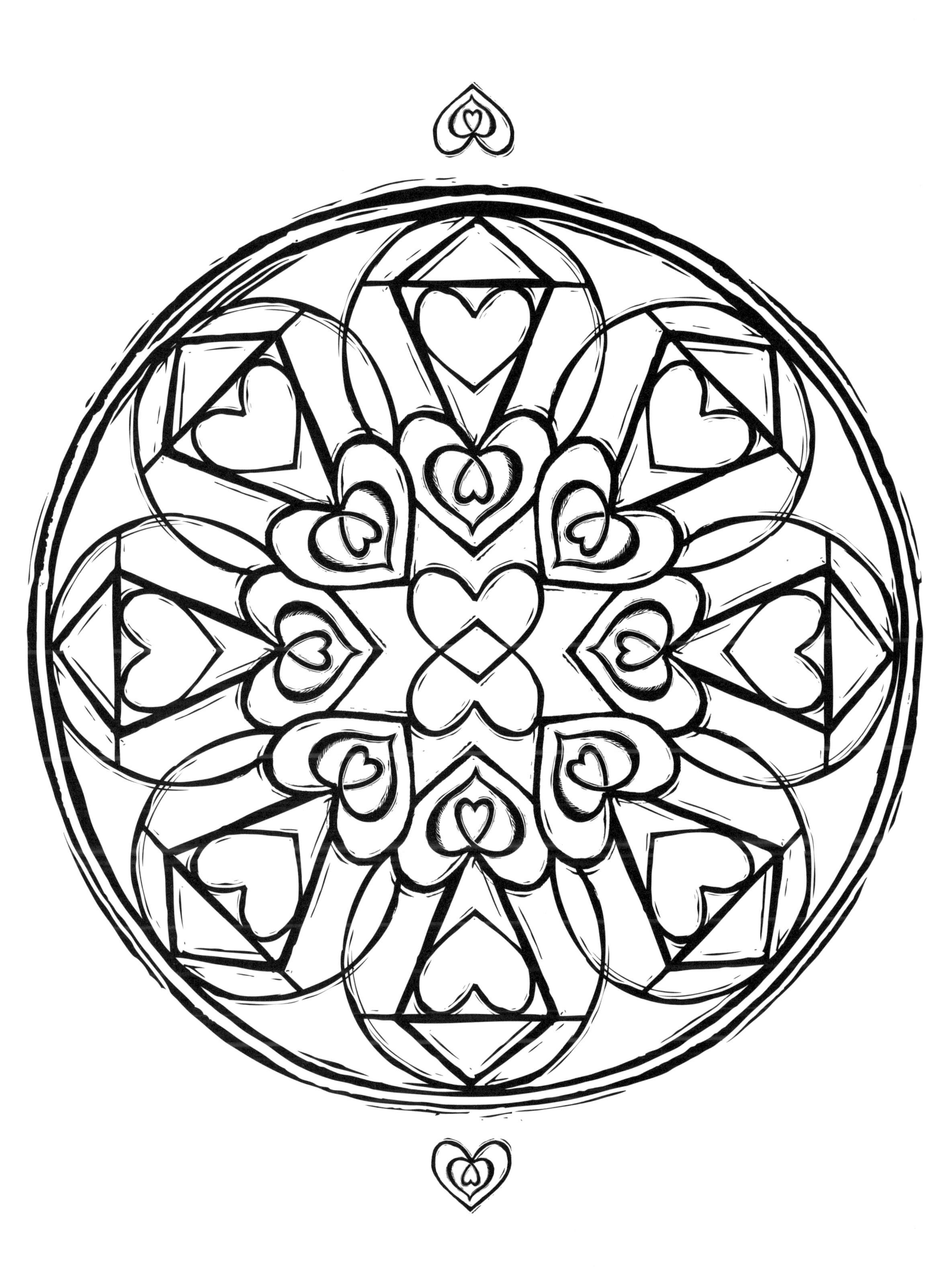

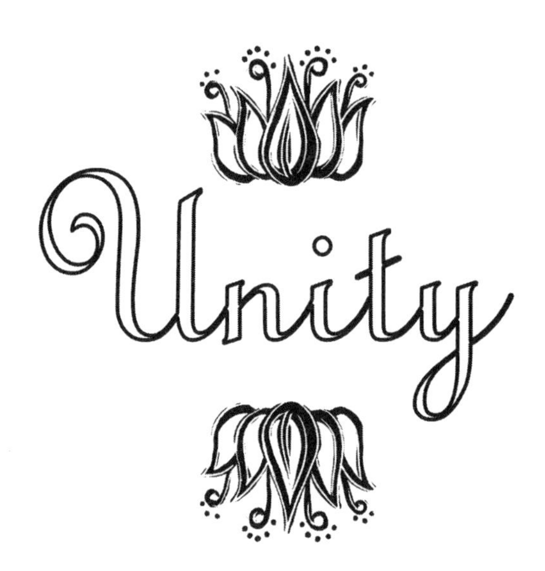
Unity

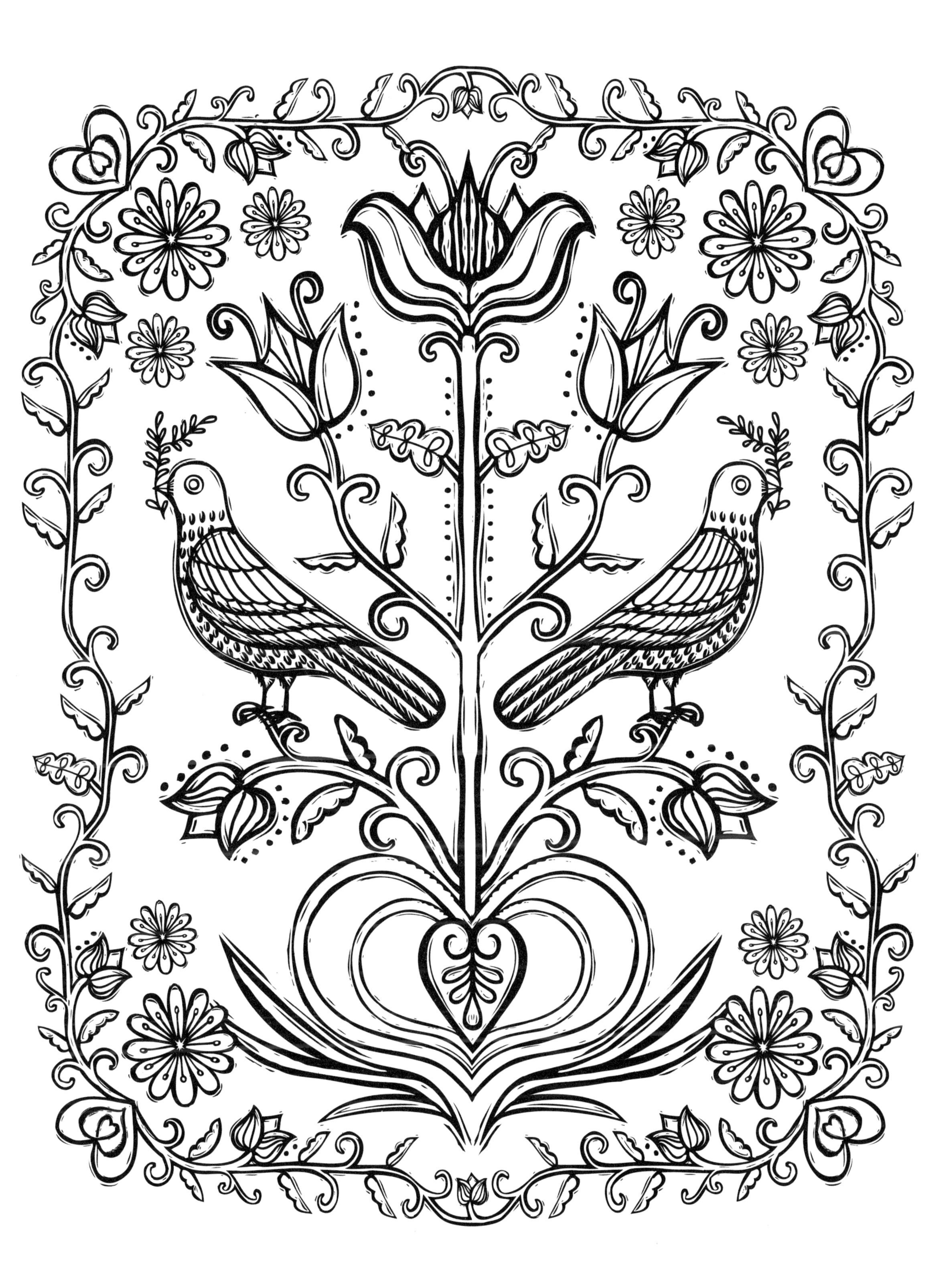

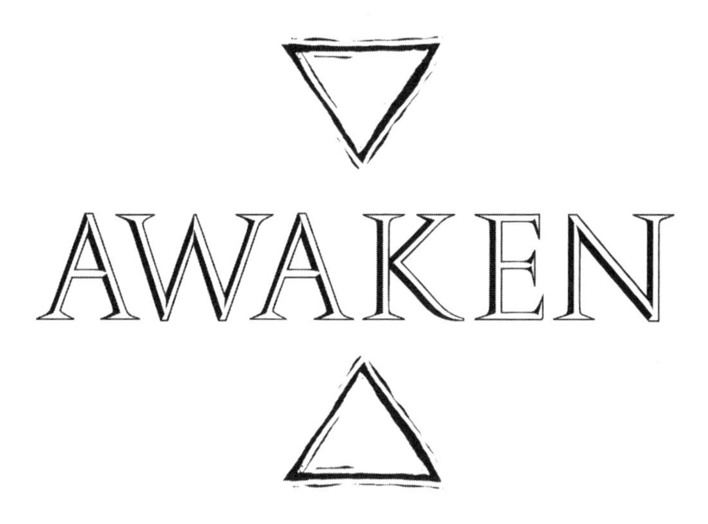
AWAKEN

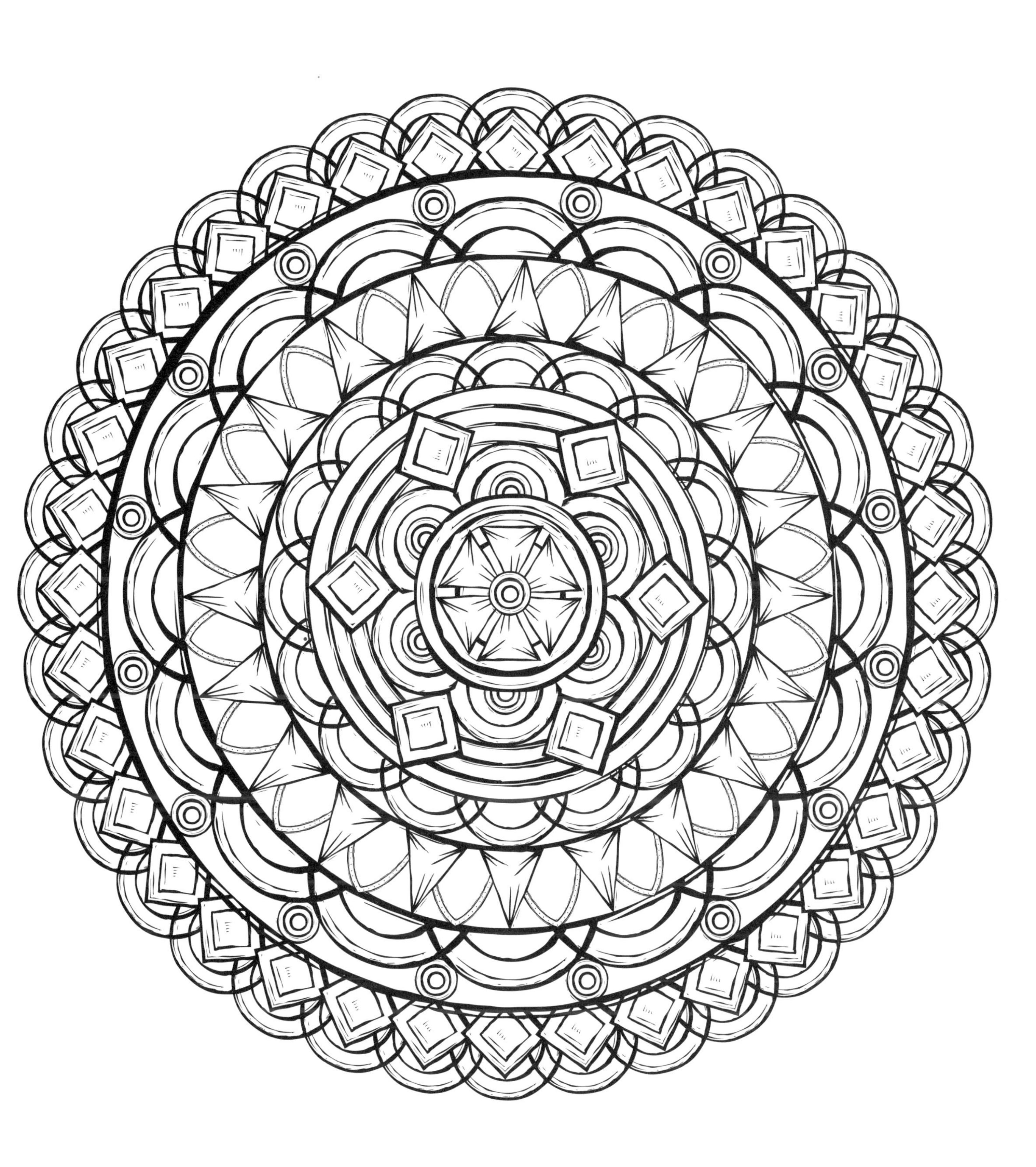

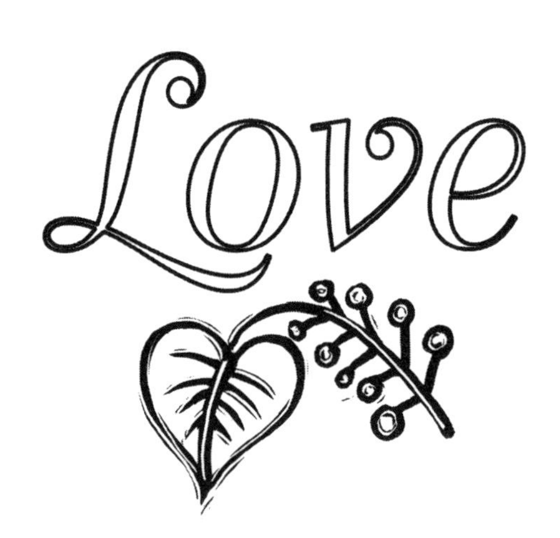
Love

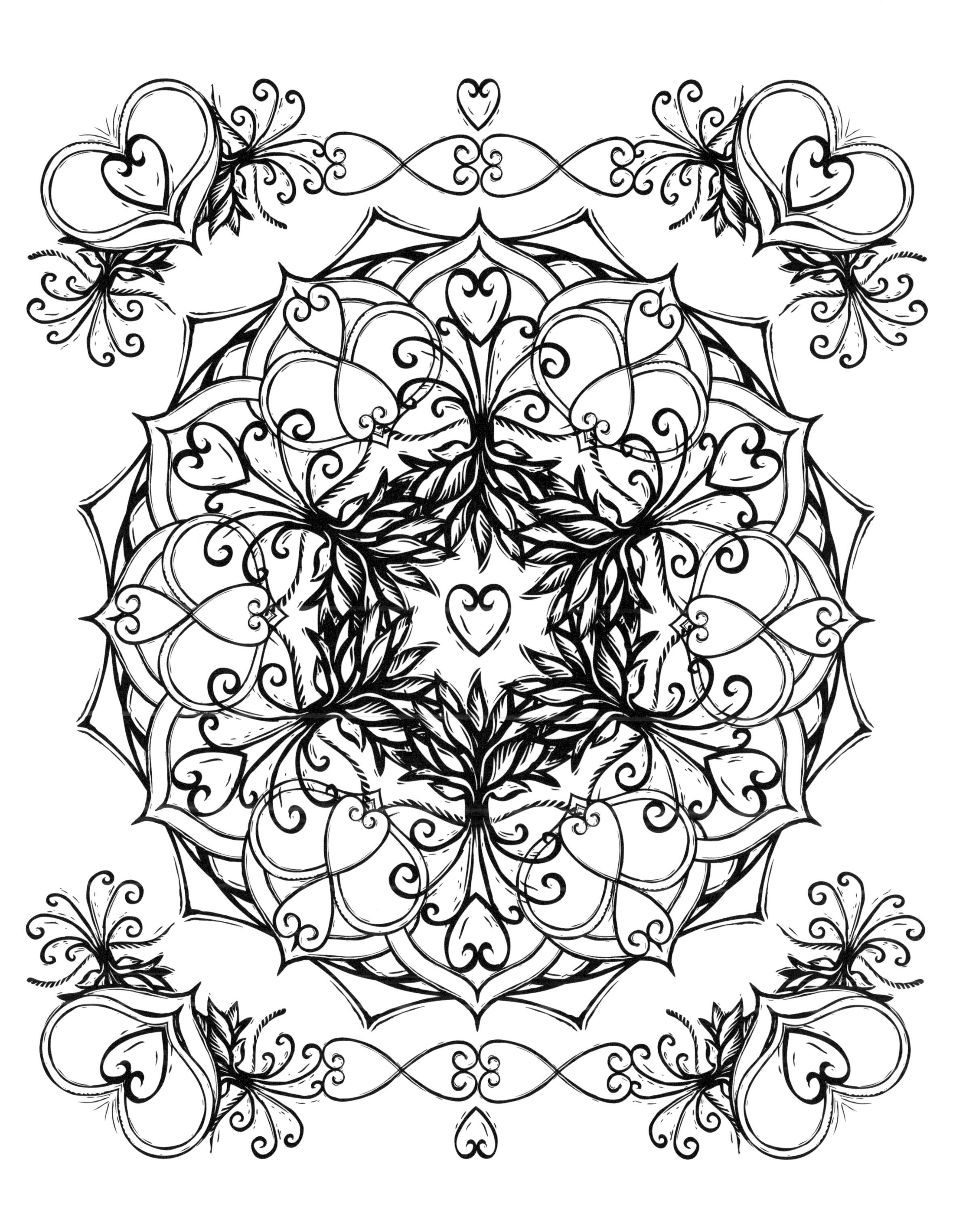

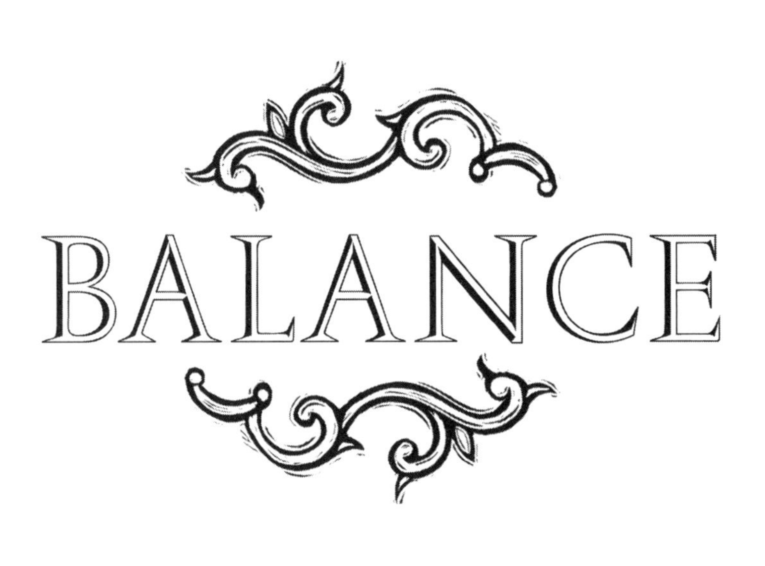
BALANCE

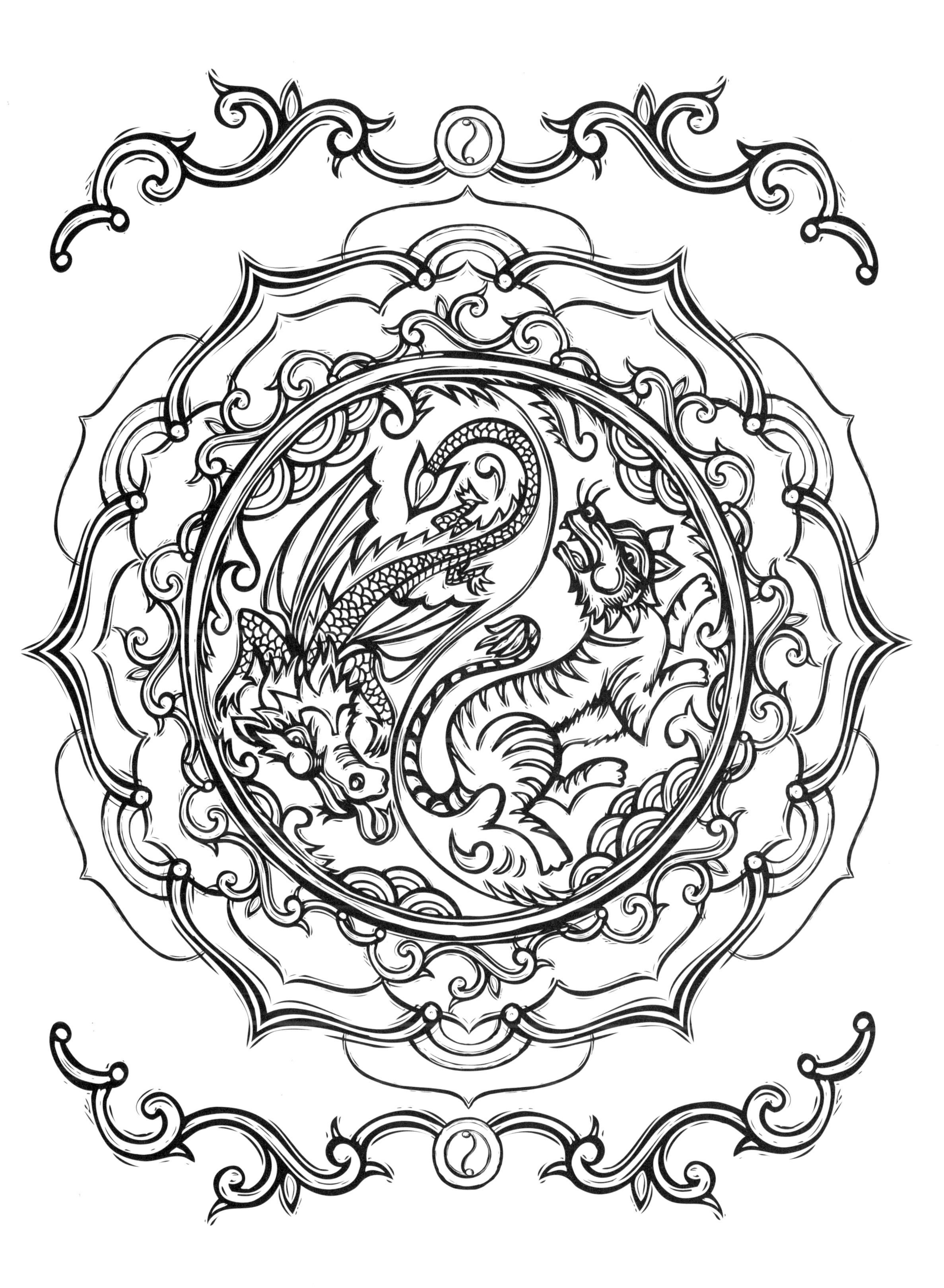

Equilibrium

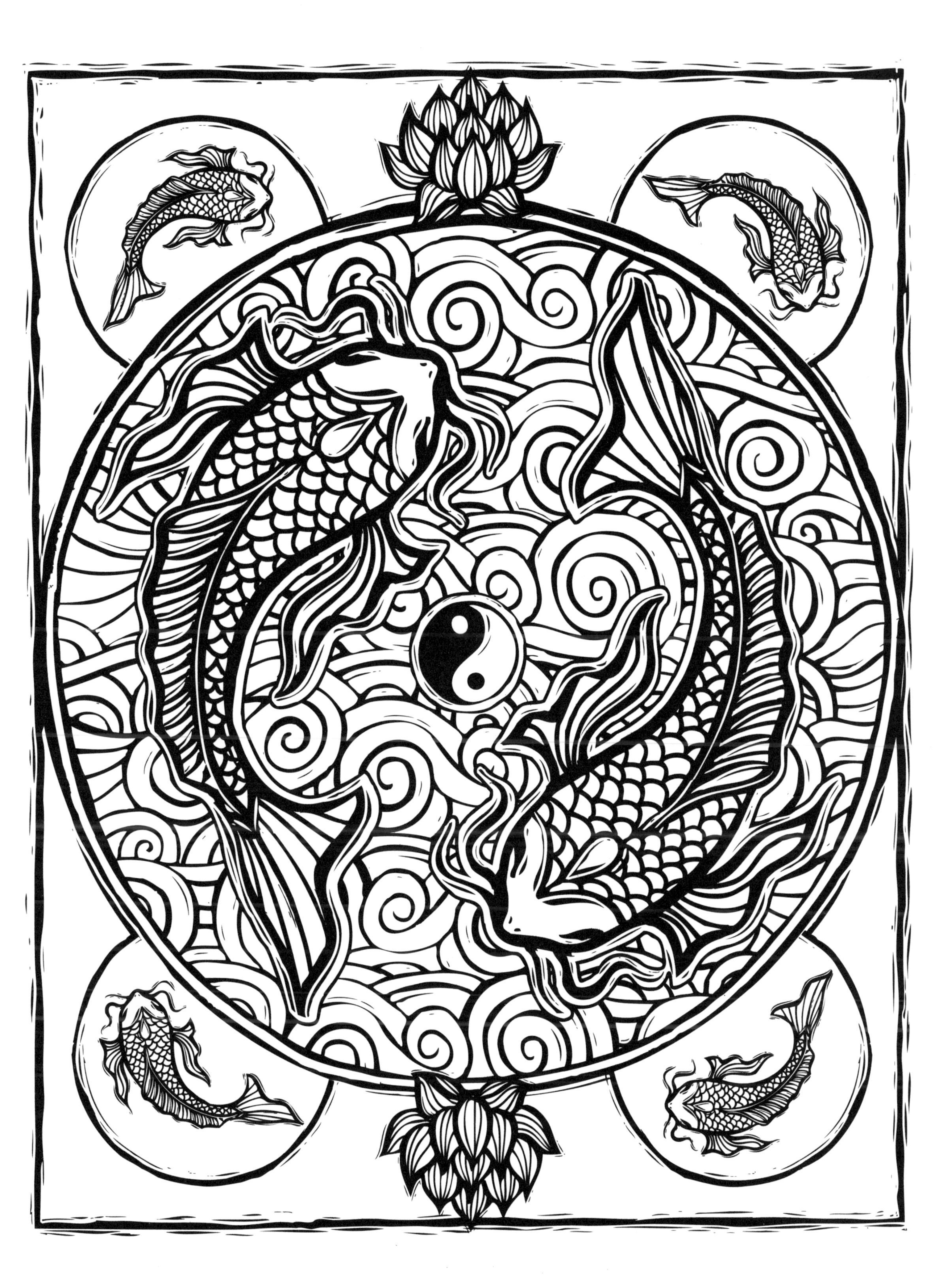

Longevity

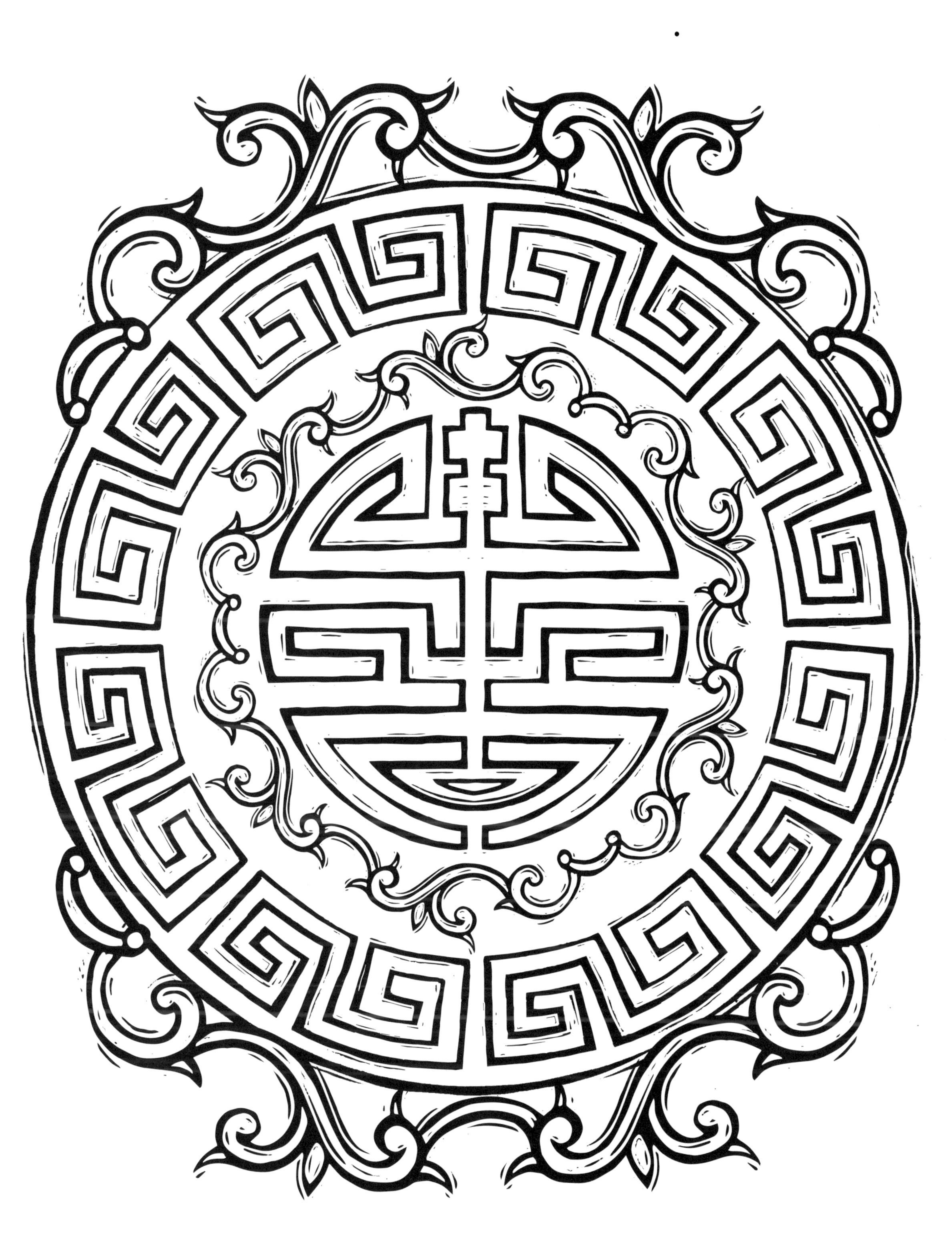

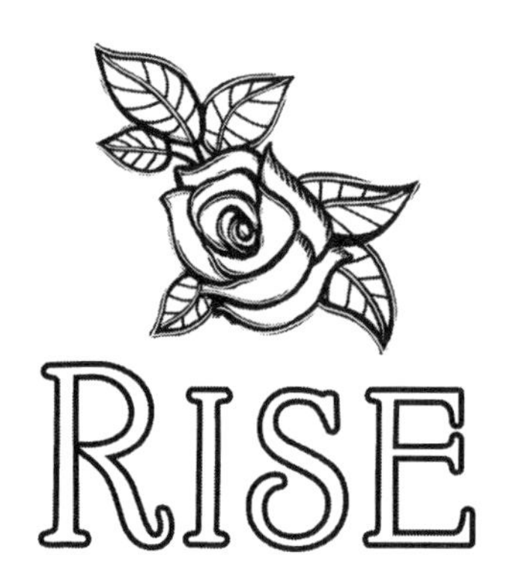
RISE

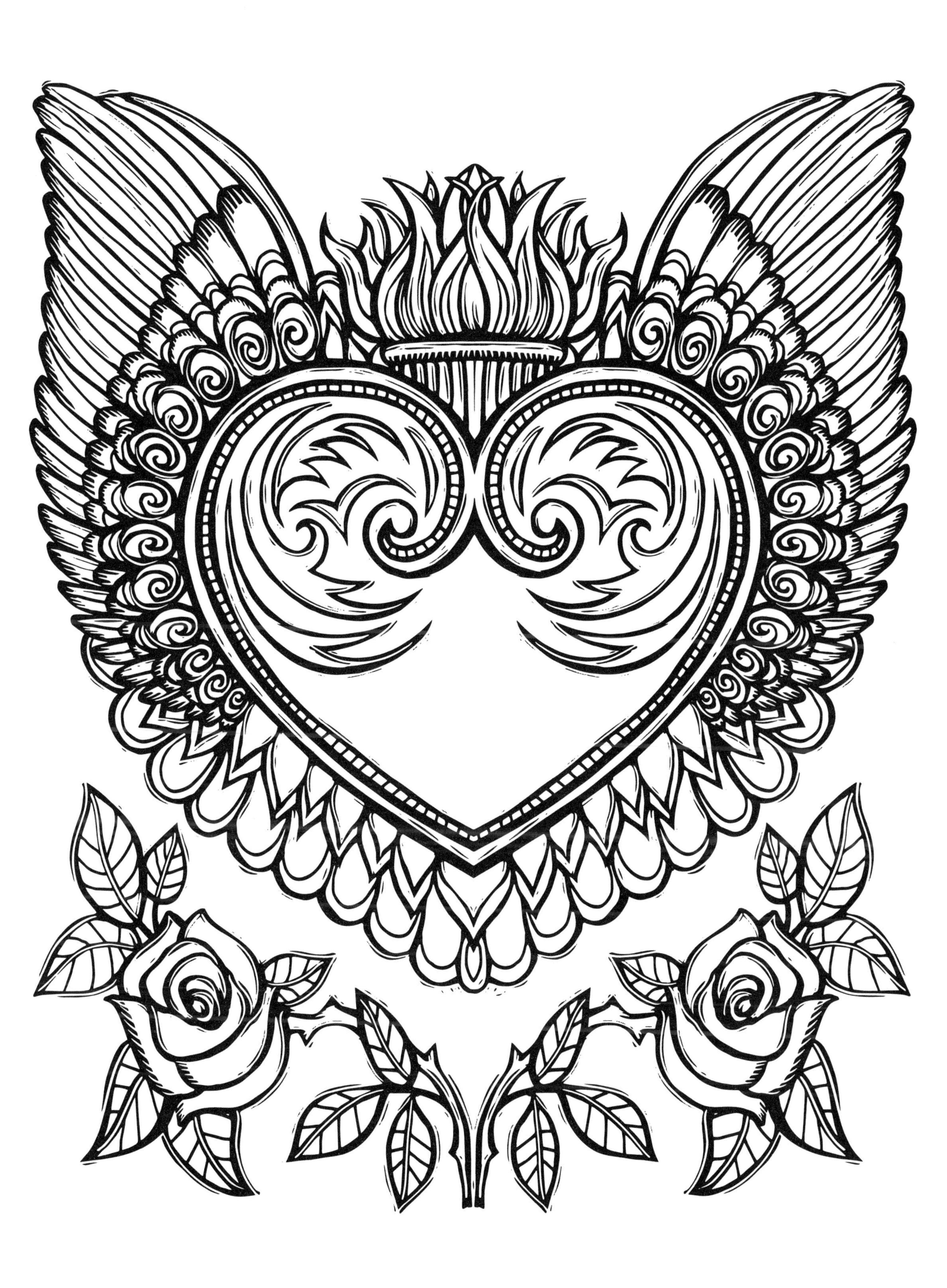

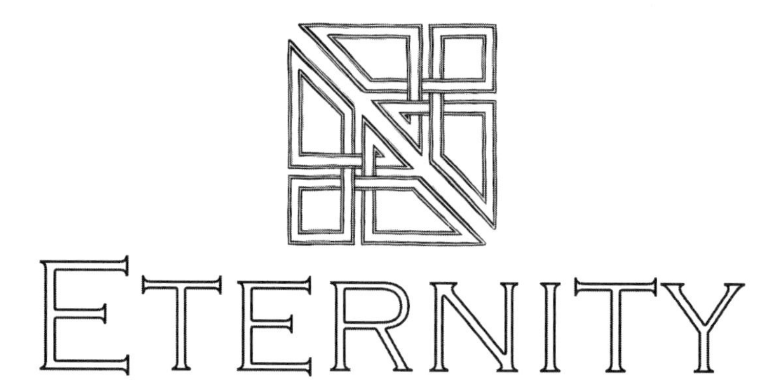
ETERNITY

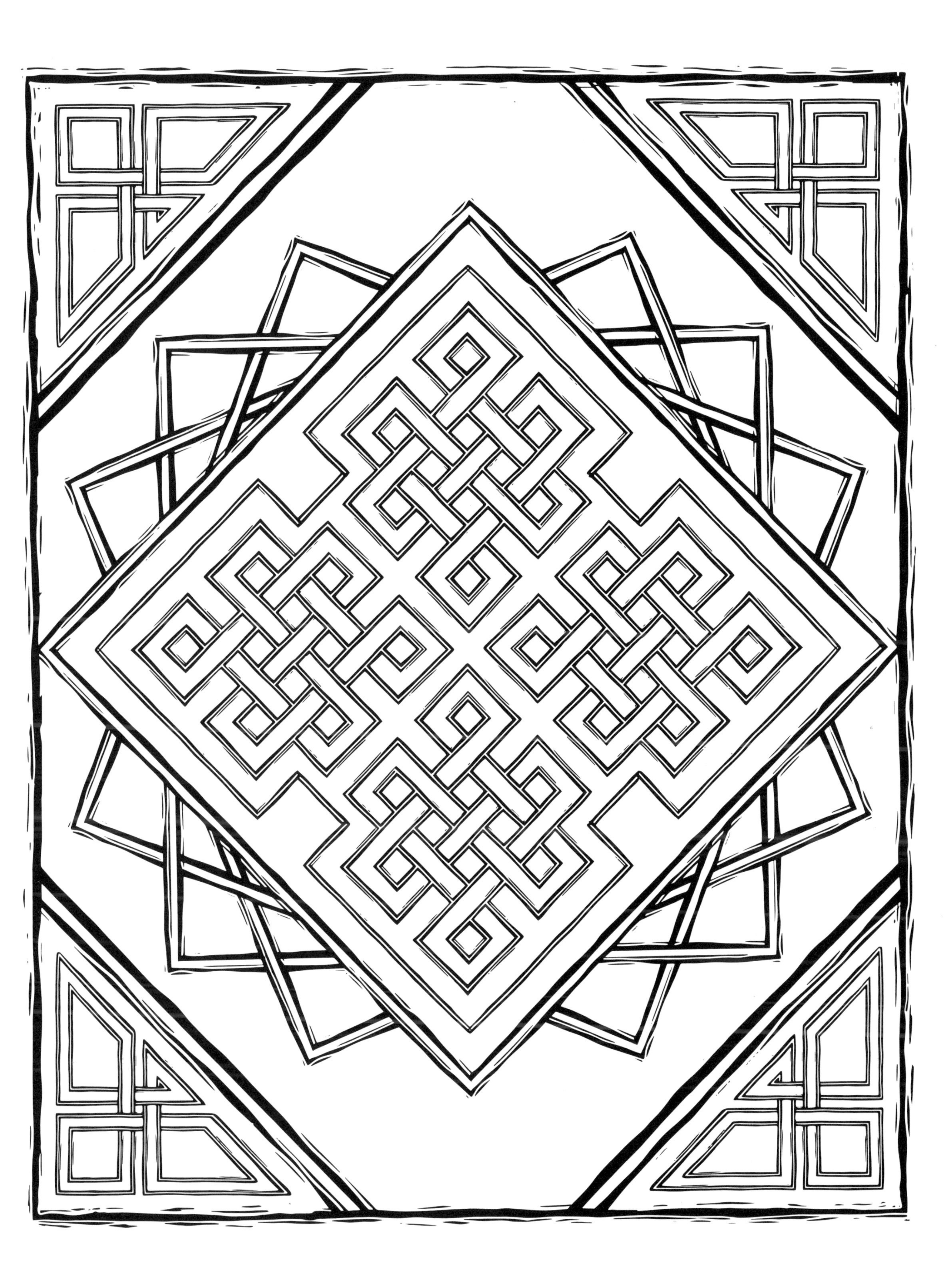

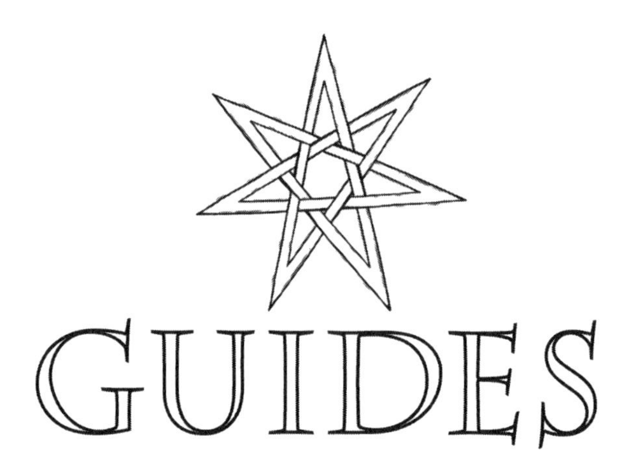
GUIDES

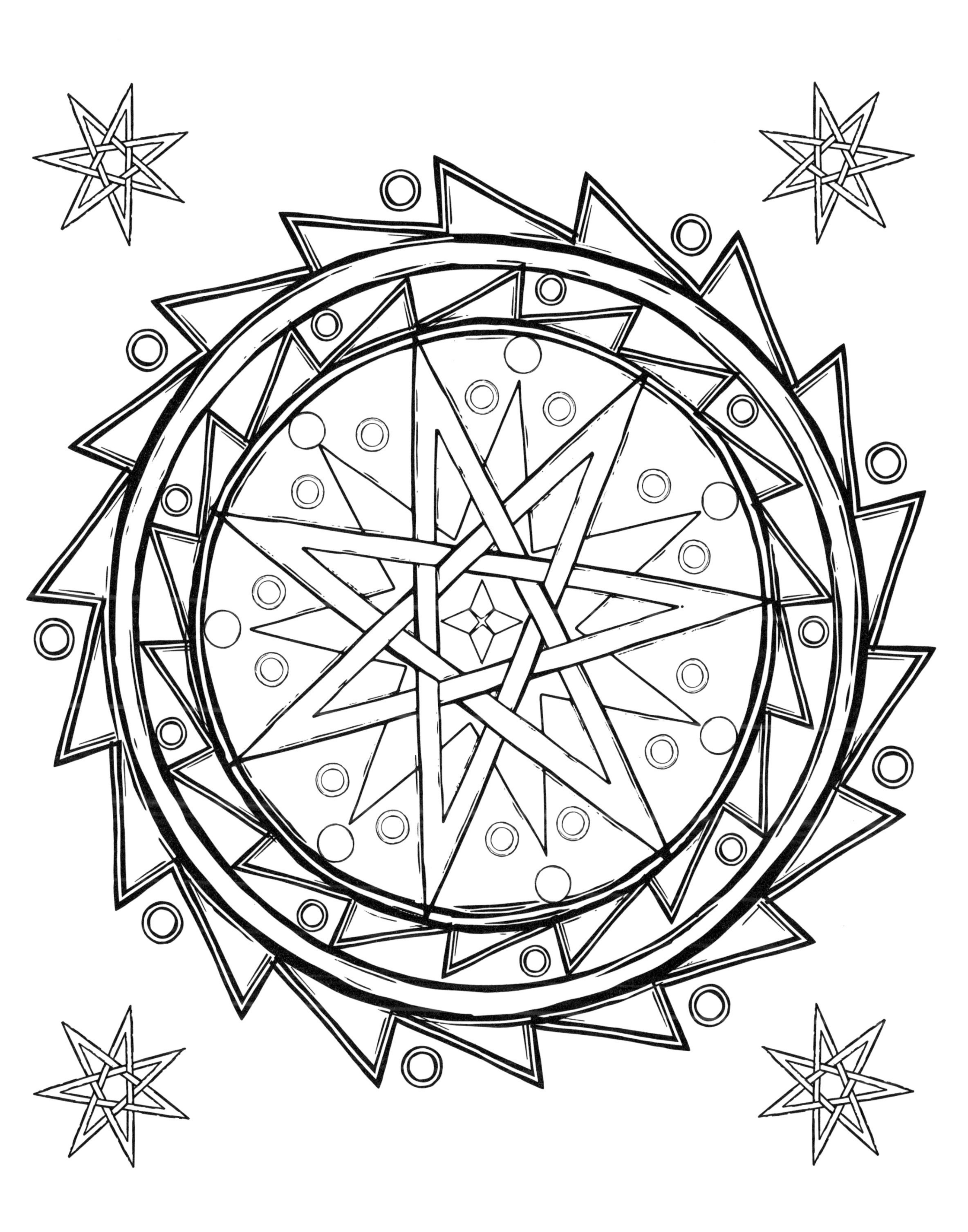

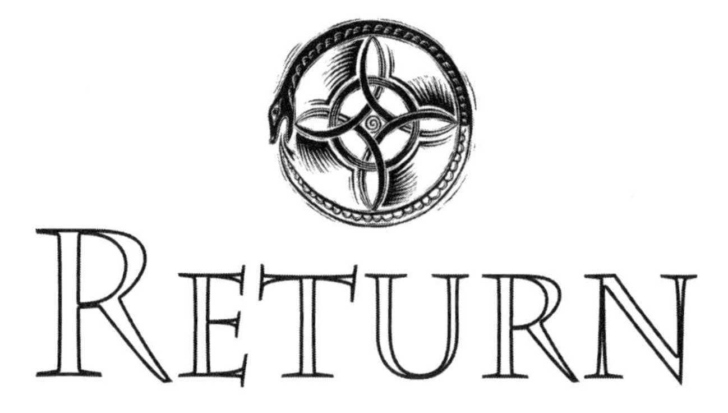
RETURN

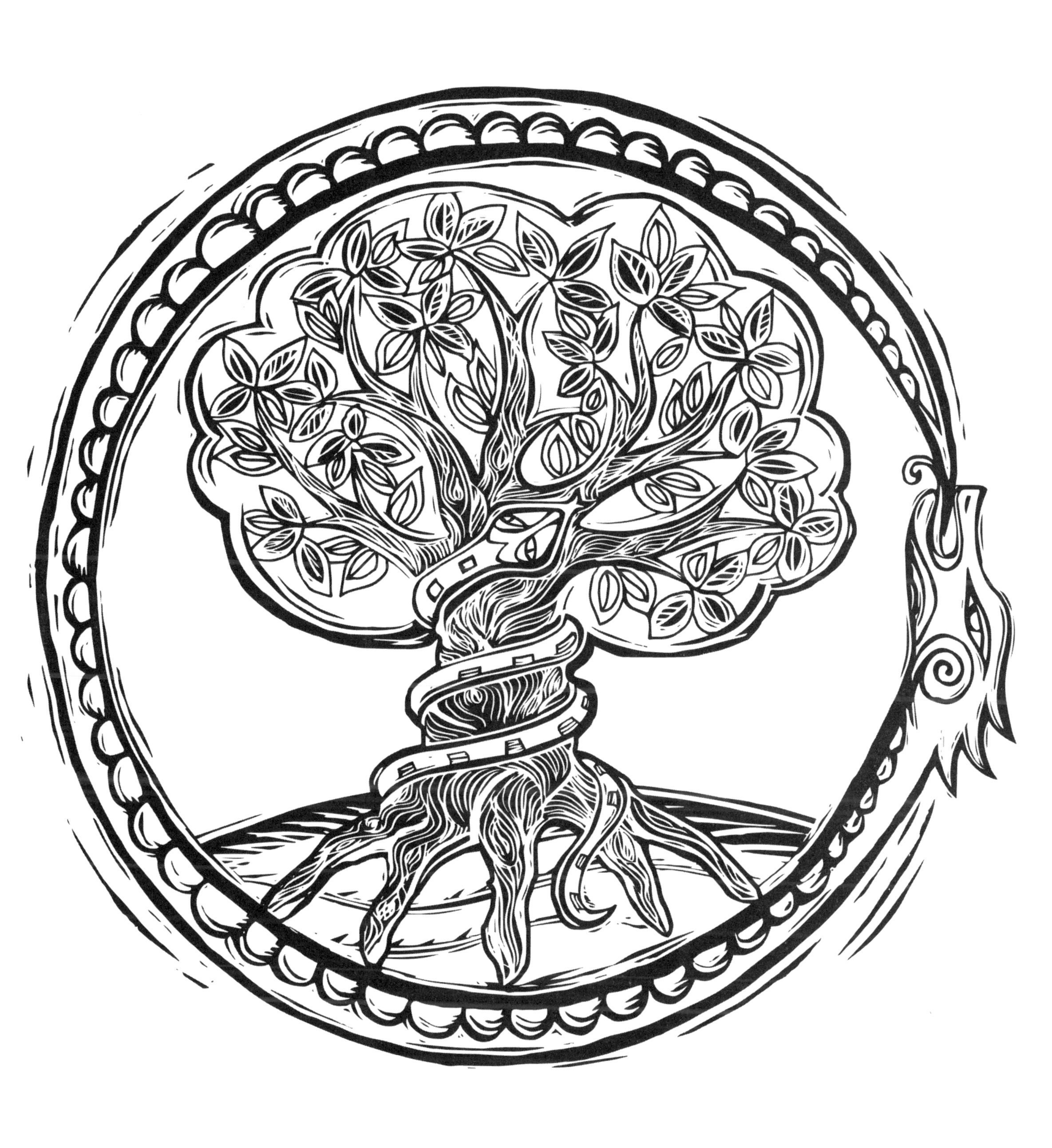

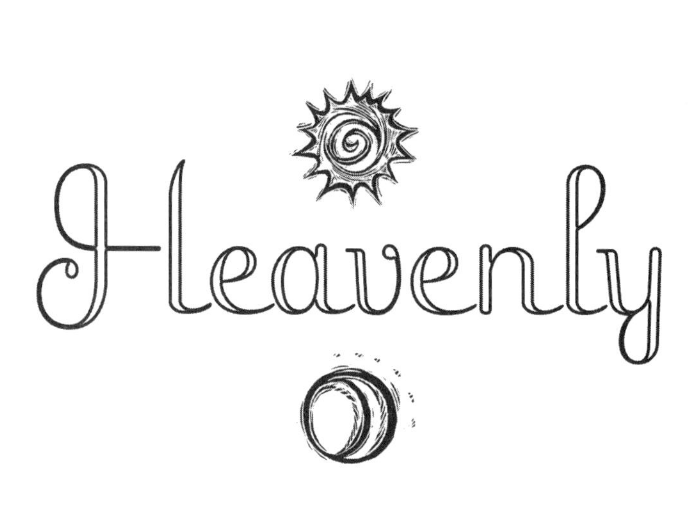
Heavenly

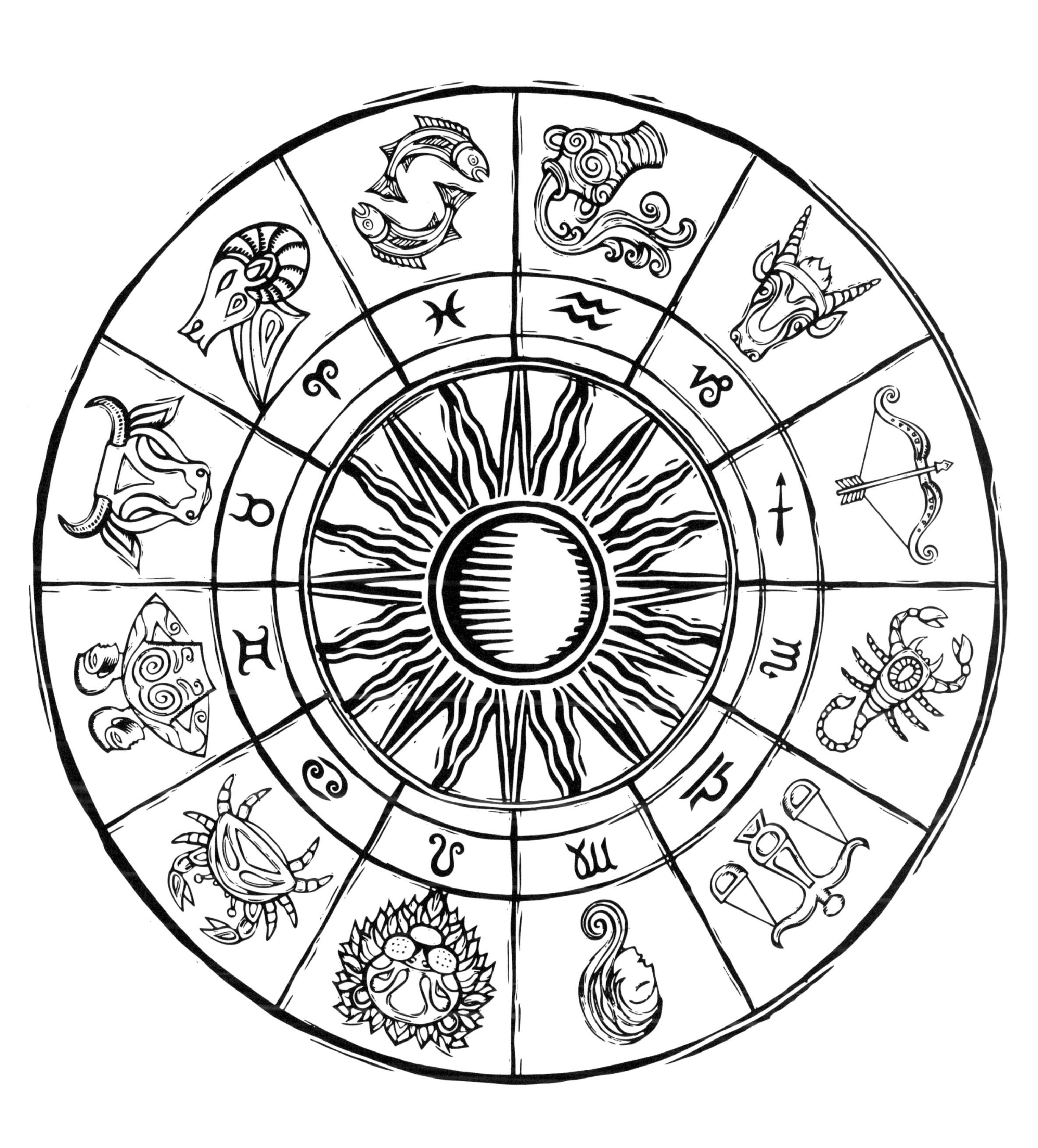

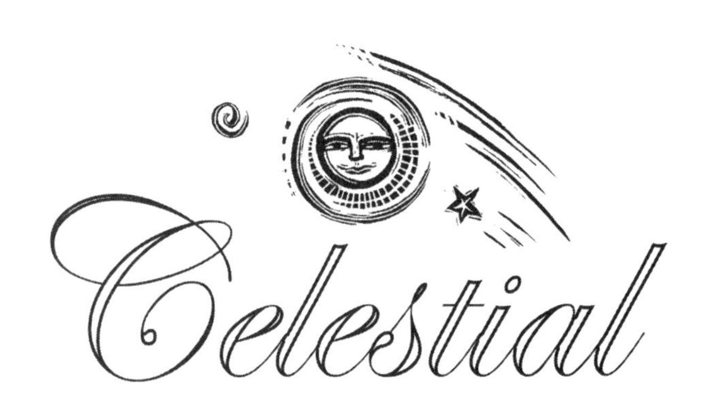
Celestial

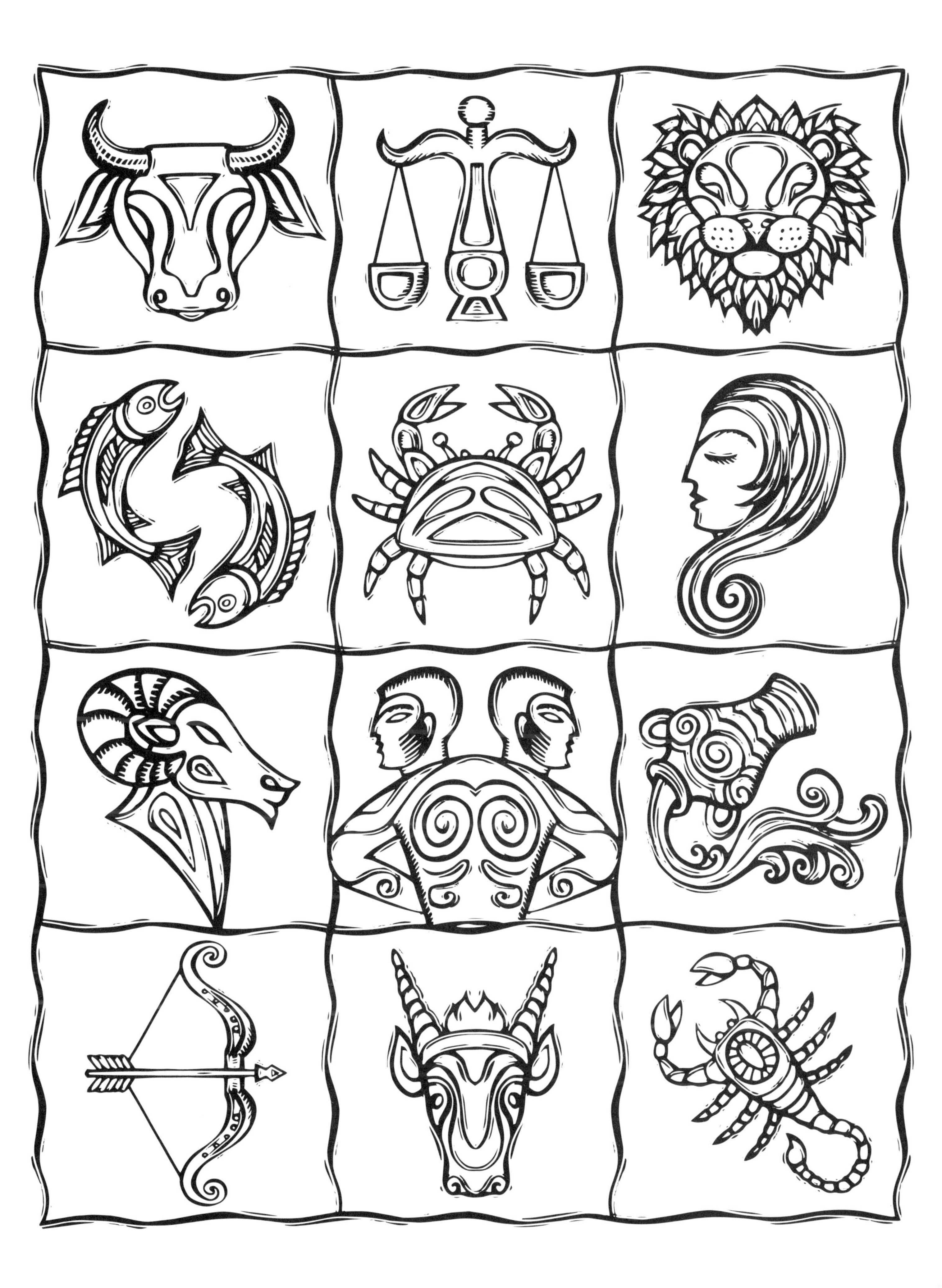

Expansion

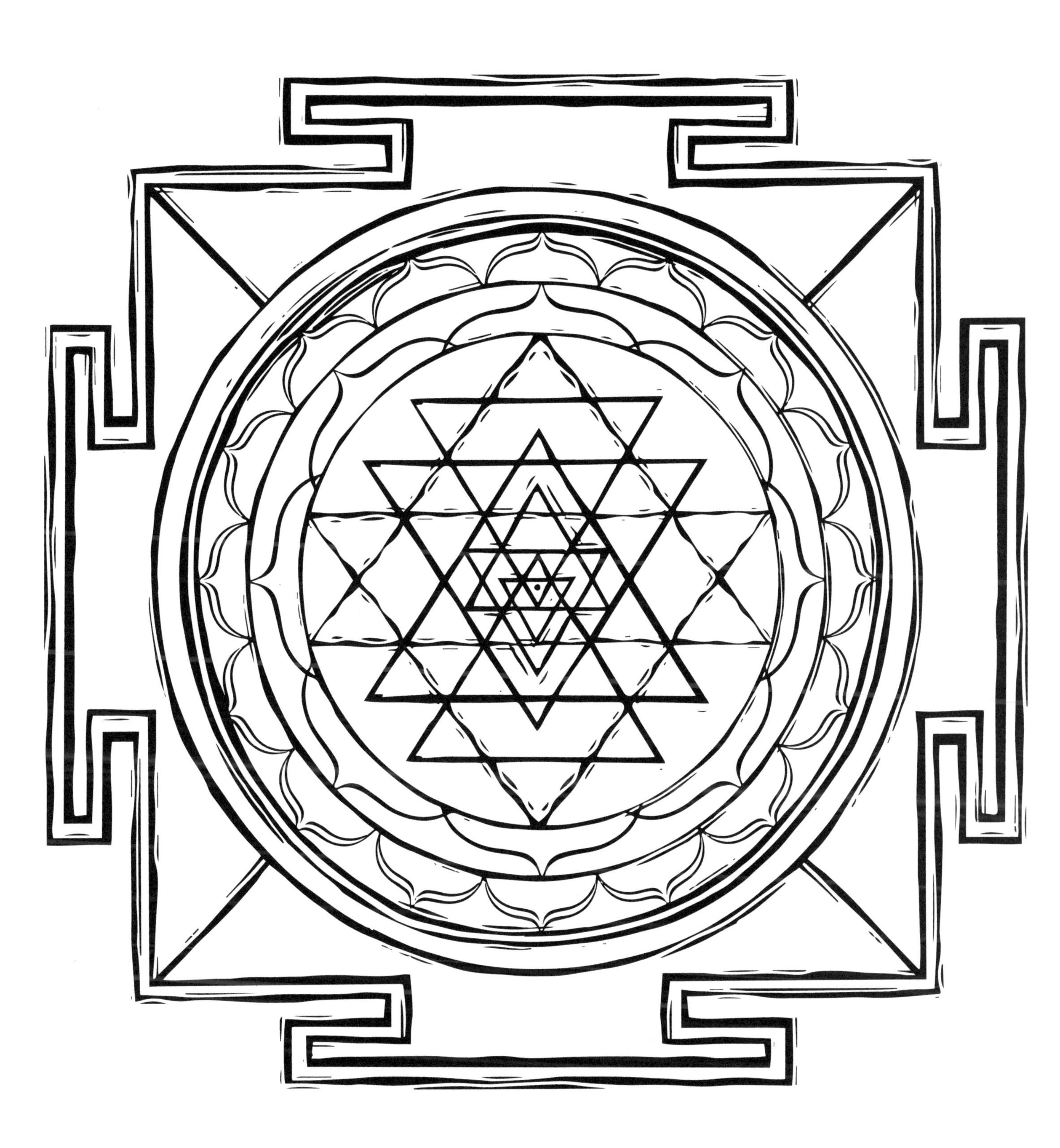

Journey

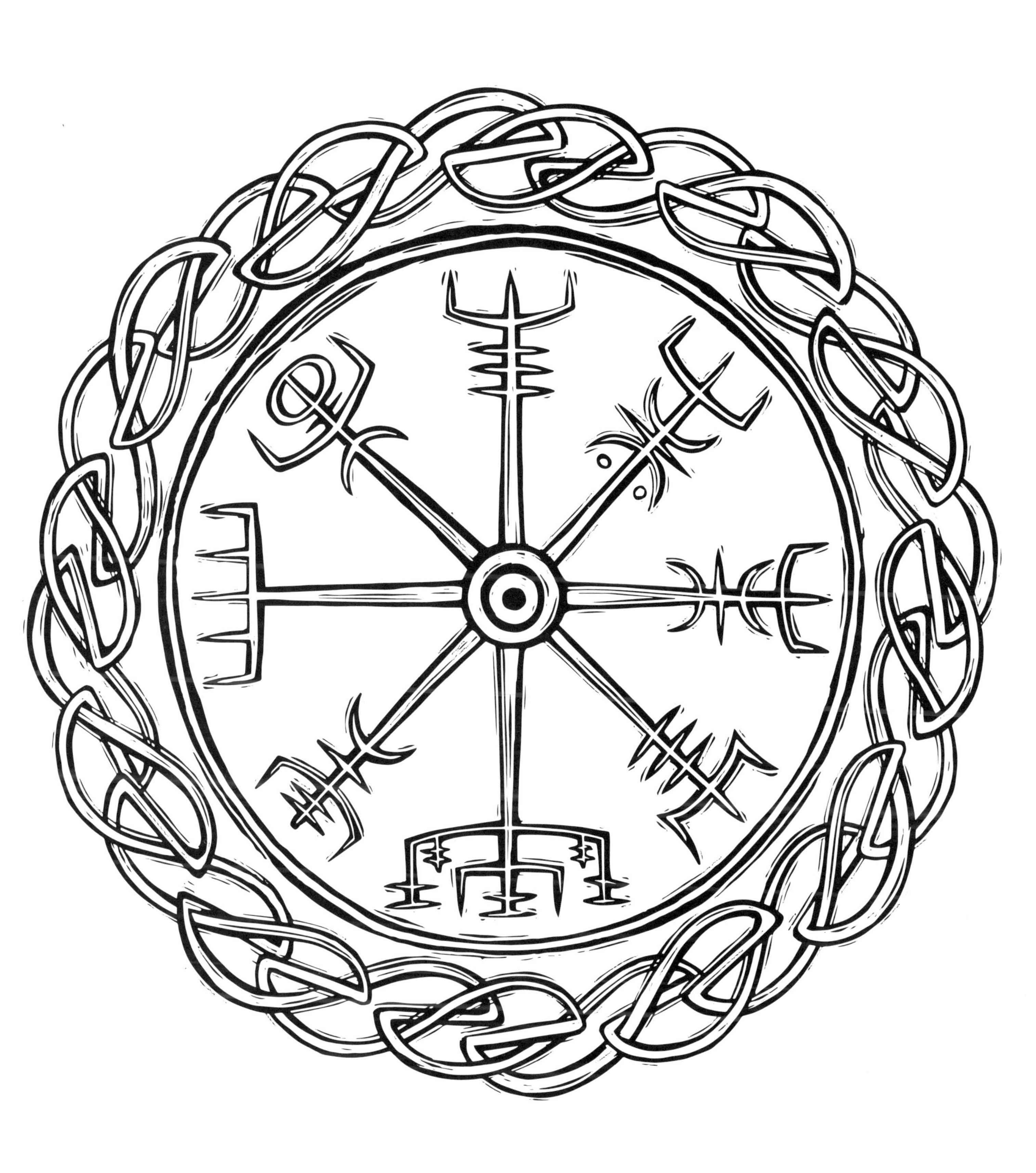

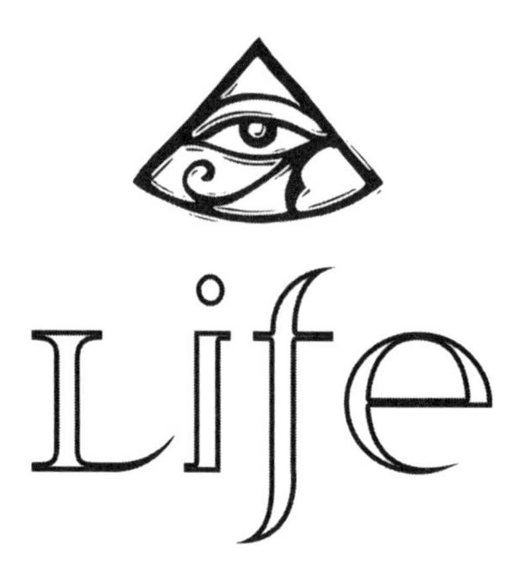
Life

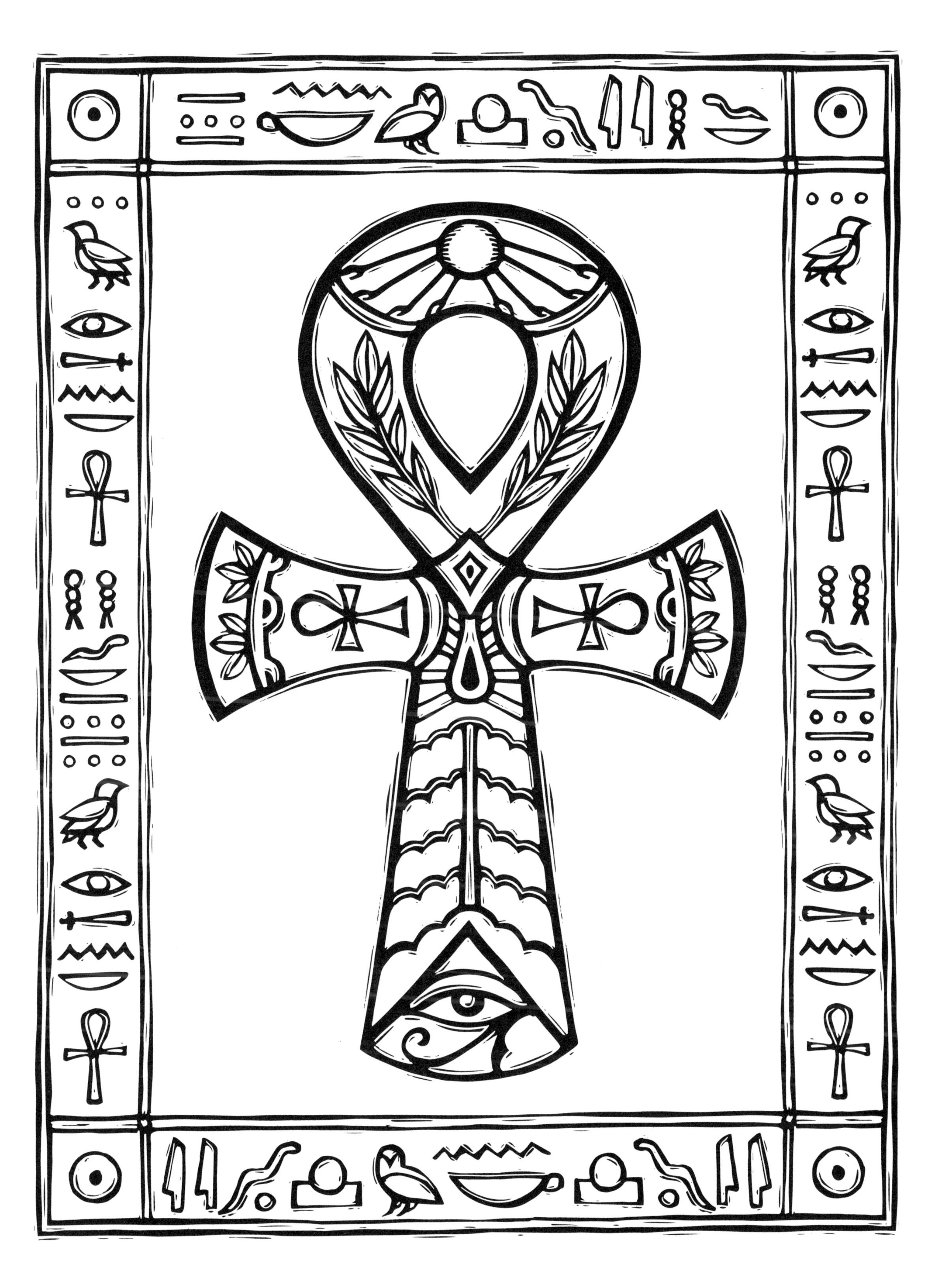

enlighten

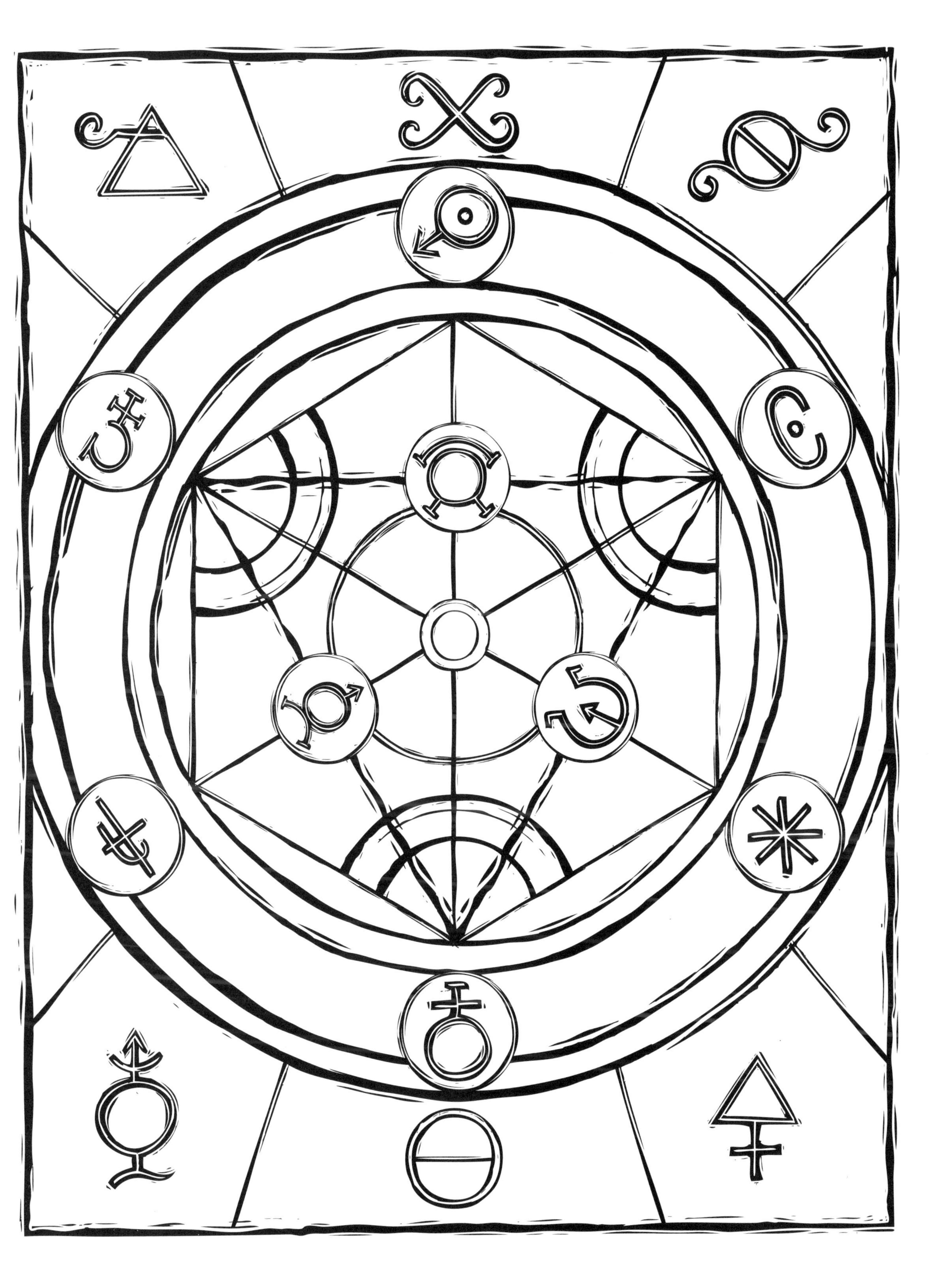

QUEST

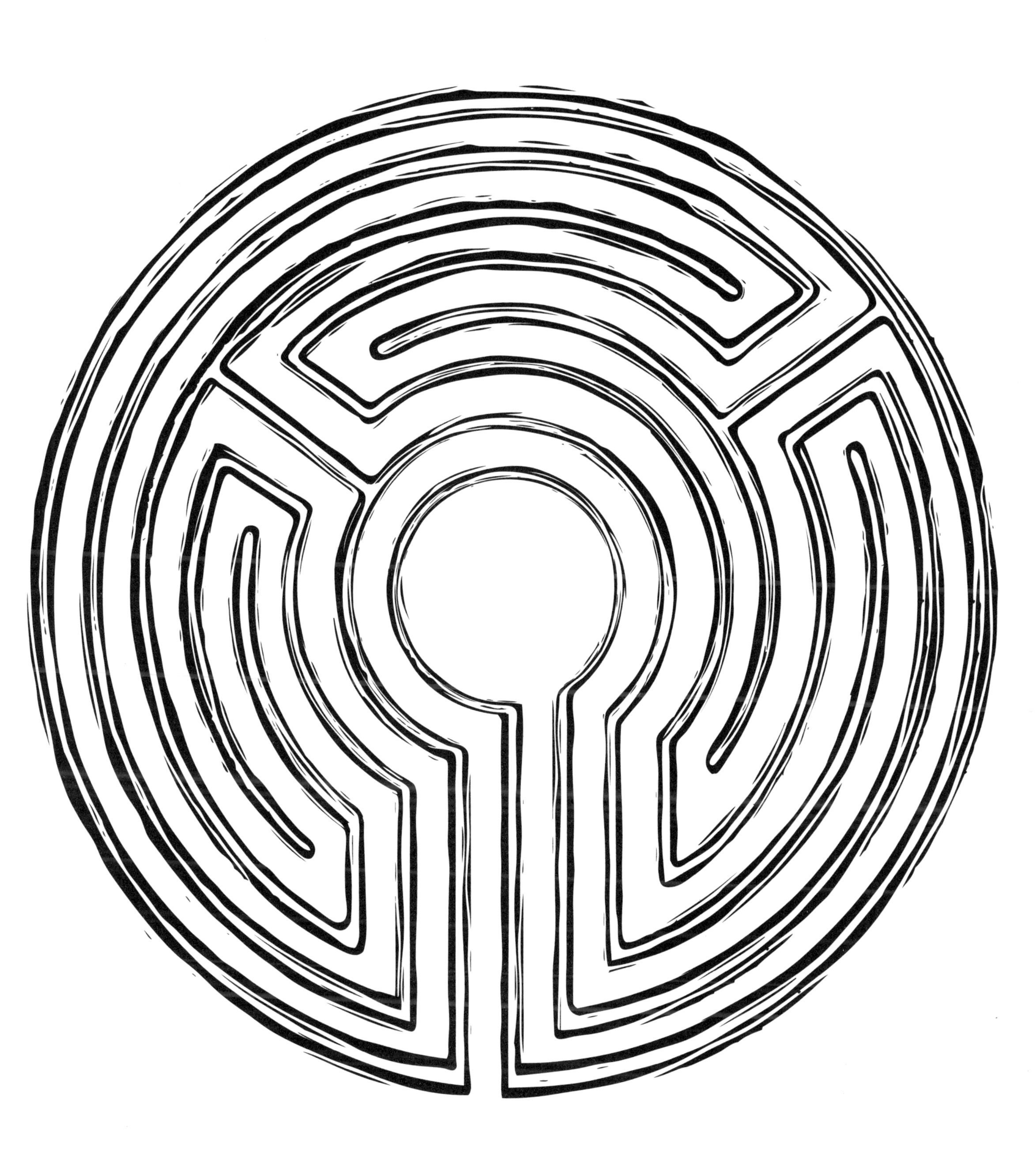

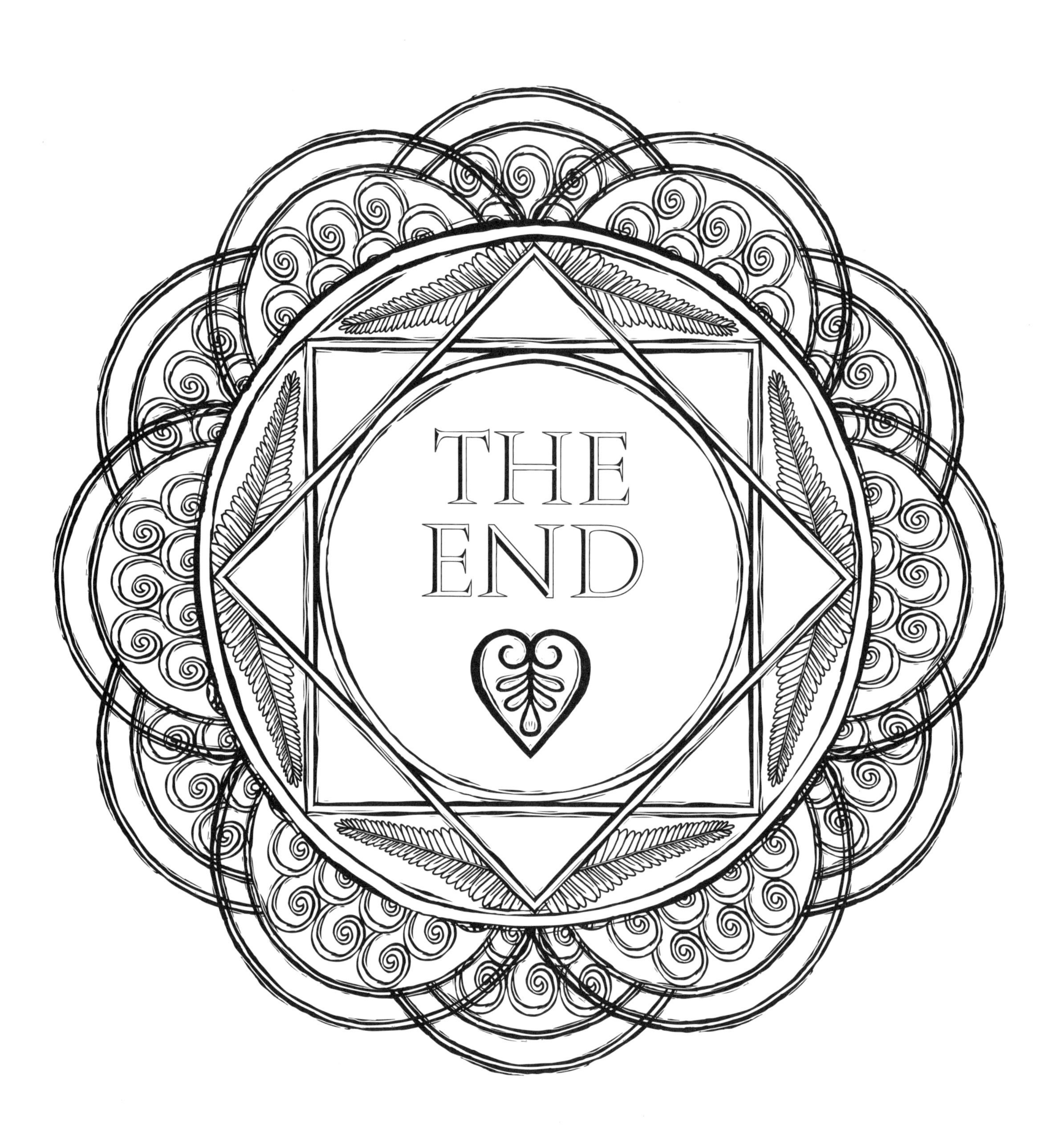
THE
END